MANAGING
TRANSITIONS

2nd Edition
Updated and
Expanded

Other Books by William Bridges

Transitions

Jobshift

Surviving Corporate Transition

The Character of Organizations

A Year in the Life

Creating You & Co.

The Way of Transition

MANAGING TRANSITIONS

2nd Edition Updated and Expanded

TRANSITIONS

Making the Most of Change

WILLIAM BRIDGES

PERSEUS
PUBLISHING

A Member of the Perseus Books Group

Library of Congress Control Number: 2003103476
ISBN 0–7382–0824–8

Perseus Publishing is a Member of the Perseus Books Group.
Find us on the World Wide Web at http://www.perseuspublishing.com
Perseus Publishing books are available at special discounts for bulk purchases in the U.S. by corporations, institutions, and other organizations. For more information, please contact the Special Markets Department at the Perseus Books Group, 11 Cambridge Center, Cambridge, MA 02142, or call (800) 255–1514 or (617) 252–5298, or e-mail j.mccrary@perseusbooks.com.

Text design by Trish Wilkinson
Set in 11-point Adobe Garamond by Perseus Publishing Services

First printing, May 2003

1 2 3 4 5 6 7 8 9 10—06 05 04 03

Contents

Acknowledgments

When the first edition of this book was published, I acknowledged the help that other consultants and workers in client organizations had given me when I was learning how transition affects organizations and what can be done to make transition less destructive. In the dozen years since the book was originally published, my associates and I have had the chance to refine our approach by helping several hundred organizations use transition management strategies to smooth the path of their reorganizations, mergers, leadership changes, culture shifts, and changes in strategy. And again, the people in those organizations and their consultants were generous with their assistance—both with the projects and with teaching me about the way transition can be not only contained but even harnessed for growth.

Many of these projects and most of the public qualification seminars that my firm conducted during those years were in the skilled hands of my two longtime associates Chris Edgelow and Ruth Morton. They were two of the first people I trained in the management of transition, and they both developed their own refinements on my original methods. I learned a great deal from watching and listening to them.

For the past several years I have been rethinking my own work with individuals and organizations in transition. A major influence during this time has been the work—and the simple presence—of my wife and business partner, Susan Mitchell Bridges. She helped me see the role that coaching and consulting can play in a practice previously based on training, and she also represents the outcome of a profound transition in my own life. I am grateful for everything that she has given me.

In our office, the business manager, Bonnie Carpenter, provided the solid infrastructure and personal support that made our far-flung and constantly evolving work go smoothly. I appreciate her help, especially since our own operations were themselves changing during that time. (We got a dose of our own medicine, so I have some experience from the other side of the organizational-transition desk.)

Jim Trupin has been my agent and friend for more than twenty years now, and he steered this project to fulfillment, as he has all of my books during those years.

In the first edition, I thanked my editor at Addison-Wesley Publishing Company, but (through one of those darned "organizational transitions"!) the book has since migrated to Perseus Publishing. That brought me a new editor, Marnie Cochran, a skilled professional who has been a pleasure to work with.

To all of these people, and the countless others who have been part of the transition management projects my firm has worked with over the years, I send my thanks.

Introduction

Diseases always attack men when they are exposed to change.
—HERODOTUS, GREEK HISTORIAN (FIFTH CENTURY B.C.)

I began my career teaching literature to undergraduates. Being twenty-five years old at the time, I felt that I understood a number of things that my elders didn't grasp. As a member of the college's Academic Policy Committee, I was also in a position to put some of my ideas into action.

Being not too far beyond student status myself, I knew how depressing it was to go to classes on Saturday. If you are old enough, you'll remember that back in the sixties most colleges had Monday-Wednesday-Friday classes and Tuesday-Thursday-Saturday classes. Students hated the latter, and some even chose their majors on the basis of which fields did not require Saturday classes.

The case against the Saturday classes was so clear, I felt, that a person had to be really stupid not to see it at a glance. First, many students skipped their Saturday classes whenever possible, and that led to gaps in their knowledge at the end of the term. Second, quite a few teachers hated them too. Third, Saturday classes required that college buildings be kept lighted and heated for an extra day every week. Fourth (and not unrelated to the third reason), the college president wanted to do away with Saturday classes. And finally, some subjects naturally lent themselves to two longer classes, which could be grouped on Tuesday and Thursday. Case closed, as far as I was concerned.

Some of the senior members of the Academic Policy Committee disagreed. They wanted to know the actual percentage of students favoring the change. ("Just about everyone" wasn't exact enough for them.) They spoke at some length about how *they* had spent their undergraduate years taking classes on Saturday, and it hadn't hurt them! ("Depends on how you define 'hurt,'" whispered another young teacher beside me.)

Just as I was about to protest, one of my elders said with exasperation, "If we shifted from three classes a week to two, I'd have to rewrite my lecture notes!" I still remember my shock as I watched most of the other committee members nod and vote down the change. As the discussion degenerated into chitchat, I searched for an explanation. Were these people self-serving hypocrites who only pretended to be interested in helping students learn? Or were they so reactionary that they would oppose any policy change automatically? Or were they simply stupid?

I think that this incident was the beginning of my lifelong interest in organizational change and why it does not happen, even when logic and common sense seem to be on its side. When I subsequently returned for my doctorate, I chose a thesis topic related to societal change. And now, forty years later, I am an organization consultant specializing in helping people through change.

Looking back at that early experience with curricular change, I'd say now that those other professors were not simply self-serving reactionaries—at least no more so than the executives and managers I work with today, or than I myself. What they were doing was the same thing that those managers and executives do—and that the college president was doing worrying about utility bills, that the students were doing trying to reclaim their Saturdays, and that I was doing trying to show my elders that they were wrong: they were struggling to protect *their world* and the meaning and identity they got from it. In the years since then, I have learned how self-defeating it is to try to overcome people's resistance to change without addressing the threat the change poses to their world.

Today this tendency leads to a serious problem: since changes are coming thick and fast, there's less and less time to let people get comfortable with them. And making changes has never been more important than it is today. Industries are consolidating, and the last one in is a loser. Technology is transforming how business is done, and holding on to the familiar old ways will leave an organization out in the cold. The other firms in the field have restructured and slimmed down and outsourced and abbreviated their products' time-to-market drastically. Their competitors can't *not* change.

And these changes cannot be delayed until everyone feels comfortable with them. An organization must be able to take changes from an initial idea to a full-scale implementation without all those little delays that used to give people time to adjust themselves and settle gradually into the new way of doing things. Change is the name of the game today, and organizations that can't change quickly aren't going to be around for long.

So what are you supposed to do? You've explained the change to every interested party and made "the case for change" repeatedly. You find yourself thinking wistfully about the old days when bosses just told people what to do—and they did it. But then it occurs to you that their response was simple *compliance.* You realize that employees in today's organizations must do more than follow orders. People have to think for themselves, function effectively without close supervision, be creative, and go the extra mile for the customer. People have to bring their hearts and their minds to work. The way change was managed in the past was designed for a time when it was sufficient to get warm bodies on the production line.

I realize that I may be in danger of losing you with this kind of talk. I may be making the management of change sound impossibly difficult. Maybe managing people isn't your strong suit. You're better at functional responsibilities and technical tasks. You don't have the skills or training to be some kind of a psychologist. You don't want to get into all that personal stuff. You just want to get results.

I sympathize. But twenty-five years of working with people in your situation has convinced me of two things:

First, you simply cannot get the results you need without getting into at least some of "that personal stuff." The results you are seeking, as we'll see shortly, depend on getting people to stop doing things the old way and getting them to start doing things a new way. And since people have a personal connection to how they work, there is just no way to do that impersonally.

Second, it doesn't take a degree in psychology to manage people in transition successfully. You are already using psychology—every time you try to guess somebody's motive, or try to explain something convincingly, or try to figure out a tactful way to handle a difficult situation. Transition management is based on some abilities you already have and some techniques you can easily learn. It isn't an undertaking that will offend anyone's sense of personal privacy, theirs or yours. Instead, it is a way of dealing with people that makes everyone feel more comfortable.

I respect your misgivings (change wasn't my top skill area either), but I think you'll find that the things you are worrying about aren't real obstacles. I'm not saying that transition management is easy—just that you can do it. And that you don't really have a choice. If you don't know where to start, this book is for you.

Part ONE

The Problem

Chapter One

It Isn't the Changes That Do You In

The beginning of wisdom is to call things by their right names.
    —CHINESE PROVERB

*It is a terrible thing to look over your shoulder when you are trying to lead—
and find no one there.*
    —FRANKLIN DELANO ROOSEVELT, AMERICAN PRESIDENT

It isn't the changes that do you in, it's the transitions. They aren't the same thing. *Change* is situational: the move to a new site, the retirement of the founder, the reorganization of the roles on the team, the revisions to the pension plan. *Transition,* on the other hand, is psychological; it is a three-phase process that people go through as they internalize and come to terms with the details of the new situation that the change brings about.

Even though you probably won't find it in the change document, transition isn't some optional "if-you-get-around-to-it" add-on to the change; it's not icing on the cake that can be forgotten until things ease up and you've finished with the important stuff. Getting people through the transition is essential if the change is actually to work as planned. When a change happens without people going through a transition, it is just a rearrangement of the chairs. It's what people mean when they say, "Just because everything has changed, don't think that anything is different around here." It's what has gone wrong when some highly touted change ends up costing a lot of money and producing disappointing results. But as important as going through transition is to getting the results that organizations are seeking, they lack a language for talking about it.

Here's an example. Benetton, the big Italian clothing firm, came up with a promising-sounding diversification plan in 1999.[1] They decided to buy some top-notch sporting goods companies—Nordica ski boots, Kastle (later

Nordica) skis, Rollerblade in-line skates, Prince tennis rackets, and Killer Loop snowboards—with the idea that buyers of those lines could also be sold cross-marketed workout and after-workout clothing made by Benetton.

It sounded like an interesting idea, and Benetton spent almost $1 billion buying the companies. They went about things as big companies often do: by imagining that everyone would be delighted to become part of a super-successful international brand. They folded the companies into their new parent, seeking the kinds of synergies and economies of scale that are always featured in stories about acquisitions. They began by combining the sales forces and marketing groups and tightened the bonds by moving the units in question to the site of the new Benetton Sportsystem division in Bordentown, New Jersey.

The trouble was that, in the words of the man who subsequently tried to save the acquisitions after things had headed south, "the people who are in these businesses are often in them because they love that activity. . . . If you sap that, you have nothing—internally or competitively." At Rollerblade, for example, employees spent their lunch hours skating through Minneapolis's lovely lakeside parks and playing roller hockey outside the headquarters building. Benetton hadn't thought through the implications of that fact—or of the impact of terminating a large percentage of the employees, three-quarters of them at Rollerblade.

The man trying to save the acquisitions got the twenty-one survivors to move to New Jersey, but only by giving many of them raises, promotions, and a promise that if they wanted to return to Minnesota within a year of the move, they'd be moved back free and receive severance packages of up to two years. When they got to New Jersey, many of them found that they were reporting to (former) Nordica reps. (That was better than what happened to the tennis racket crew from Prince, who were all fired.) The bottom line—that mythic measure that justifies anything—was that during the year when all this happened, Benetton went from making a U.S. profit of $5 million to posting a loss of $31 million. Incidentally, twenty out of the twenty-one Rollerbladers took the company up on its offer and moved back to the Land of 10,000 Lakes.

Not all mismanaged transitions turn out so badly, but this one contains just about all the elements. Managing transition involves not just whopping financial deals but the simple process of helping people through three phases:

1. Letting go of the old ways and the old identity people had. This first phase of transition is an ending, and the time when you need to help people to deal with their losses.

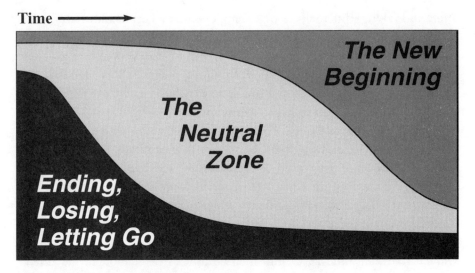

Time ⟶

The New Beginning

The Neutral Zone

Ending, Losing, Letting Go

Figure 1.1 **The three phases of transition.**

2. Going through an in-between time when the old is gone but the new isn't fully operational. We call this time the "neutral zone": it's when the critical psychological realignments and repatterings take place.

3. Coming out of the transition and making a new beginning. This is when people develop the new identity, experience the new energy, and discover the new sense of purpose that make the change begin to work.

Because transition is a process by which people unplug from an old world and plug into a new world, we can say that transition starts with an ending and finishes with a beginning.

In its disastrous sortie into sporting goods, Benetton managed the change—combining staffs and moving them—and forgot the transition. They had a difficult ending, which the planners of the change didn't even acknowledge. The employees incurred huge psychological losses (a favored location, a corporate identity tied to an activity they loved, the esprit de corps that comes from shared interests and involvement in a cutting-edge activity), and the company treated those losses as just another cash deal. The company neither offered nor acknowledged the need for any support during the difficult neutral zone, and their notion of help in making a new beginning was new titles and higher performance targets.

Changes of any sort—even though they may be justified in economic or technological terms—finally succeed or fail on the basis of whether the people affected do things differently. Do the employees let go of the old way of doing things, go through that difficult time between the old way and the new, and come out doing things the new way? If they don't help people through these three phases, even the most wonderful training programs often fall flat. The leaders forget endings and neutral zones; they try to start with the final stage of transition. And they can't see what went wrong!

Back in the 1980s a large American insurance company launched a program to generate cost-saving ideas. I don't know what it cost, but it must have been expensive since it involved coordinating the activities and output of 485 teams. The director of the effort later reported (with no apparent awareness of the irony of what he was saying) that "the most creative idea submitted to date, and which supports the best intentions of the program, has potential annualized savings of $40,000. If paper inserted into a fax machine is inserted sideways, it will cut transition time 15%." But then he added that he thought they'd have trouble implementing the idea, "because it means changing behavior."[2]

Well, scratch that idea! Let's find one that *doesn't* mean changing behavior. All the significant ones involve changing behavior, you say? Turning the paper 90 degrees before you put it in the fax machine is a minor change compared to the behavior changes needed to make a merger, a reorganization, or a new corporate strategy work. Those changes trigger thousands of smaller changes, all of which require people to stop doing things an old way—which earned them rewards, gave them the satisfaction that comes from doing things "right," and got them the results that made them feel successful—and try new and unfamiliar behaviors.

What happens in such a case reminds me of one of my early transition management projects, which involved setting up self-managed teams in a factory. The company offered classes (pretty good ones actually) on how self-managed teams work, but they offered no help to the supervisors who had to let go of "supervising" and start "facilitating" those teams. At the end of one of these classes the instructor asked if there were any questions. "Yeah," growled a grizzled old supervisor. "Will you run that 'fassiltating thing' by me one more time?" The idea of no longer telling people what to do and punishing them when they didn't do it was so incomprehensible to the fellow that he just couldn't get his tongue around the word for what he was supposed to do in its place.

Several important differences between change and transition are overlooked when people think of transition as simply gradual or unfinished change or when they use *change* and *transition* interchangeably.[3] With a change, you nat-

The change of clothes; changed, yes, but the same lice of my journeying.

ISSA, JAPANESE POET

urally focus on the outcome that the change produces. If you move from California to New York City, the change involves crossing the country and then learning your way around the Big Apple. The same is true of your organization's change to a service culture or its reorganization into a regionally based sales force. In such cases the affected people have to understand the new arrangements and how they'll be affected by these changes.

Transition is different. The starting point for dealing with transition is not the outcome *but the ending that you'll have to make to leave the old situation behind.* Situational change hinges on the new thing, but psychological transition depends on letting go of the old reality and the old identity you had before the change took place. Organizations overlook that letting-go process completely, however, and do nothing about the feelings of loss that it generates. And in overlooking those effects, they nearly guarantee that the transition will be mismanaged and that, as a result, the change will go badly. Unmanaged transition makes change unmanageable.

Transition starts with an ending. That is paradoxical, but true. Think of a big change in your own life: getting promoted into management; moving into the first house you owned; coming home from the hospital with your first child. Good changes, all of them, but as transitions each one started with an ending and a letting go. With the job, you may have had to let go of your old peer group. They weren't peers anymore, and the kind of work you really liked may have come to an end when you shifted to managing your old peers who still did that kind of work. Perhaps you even had to give up the feeling of competence that came from doing that work. Maybe you had to let go of your old habit of leaving your work at the office when you picked up the round-the-clock responsibility of a managerial job.

With the new baby, you probably had to let go of regular sleep, of extra money, of time alone with your spouse, and maybe time alone period. You almost certainly lost the pleasure of being able to take off spontaneously whenever the two of you felt like it. And there is nothing that makes you feel like you have lost your old sense of competence more than being faced with a baby who refuses to eat or just won't stop crying.

With the move, a whole network of relationships ended. Even if you kept in touch with people in the old neighborhood, it was never quite the same. In your old home, you knew where the stores were, which doctor and dentist to go to, and which neighbor would keep an eye on the house while you were gone. In the new home, you had to let go of feeling at home for a while.

*Every new truth
which has ever been
propounded has, for a
time, caused mischief; it
has produced discomfort
and oftentimes
unhappiness; sometimes
disturbing social and
religious arrangements,
and sometimes merely by
the disruption of old and
cherished associations
of thoughts. . . . And if
the truth is very great as
well as very new, the
harm is serious.*

HENRY THOMAS BUCKLE,
BRITISH HISTORIAN

Even in these *good* changes, there are transitions that begin with endings, where you have to let go of something.[4] In saying this, I am not trying to be negative or discouraging, just realistic. The failure to identify and get ready for endings and losses is the largest difficulty for people in transition. And the failure to provide help with endings and losses leads to more problems for organizations in transition than anything else.

The organization institutes a quality improvement program, and no one foresees how many people will feel a loss in letting go of their old roles. (In one client organization where people prided themselves on being able to spot defective goods as they went by on the production line, the change to statistical process control caused one production line worker to say sadly, "Heck, anybody can do my job now. You don't need no skill anymore!") Or the organization builds a beautiful new headquarters building, and nobody foresees that many people—who'd been proud that they became a $1-billion-a-year company while housed in 14 nondescript, rented buildings—will view the new headquarters as the sign that the company they loved is gone.

Once you understand that *transition begins with letting go of something,* you have taken the first step in the task of transition management. The second step is understanding what comes after the letting go: *the neutral zone.* This is the psychological no-man's-land between the old reality and the new one. It is the limbo between the old sense of identity and the new. It is the time when the old way of doing things is gone but the new way doesn't feel comfortable yet.

When you moved into your new house, or got the promotion, or had the new baby, the change probably happened pretty fast. But that is just the external, situational change. Inwardly, the psychological transition happened much more slowly: instead of becoming a new person as fast as you changed outwardly, you found yourself struggling for a time in a state that was neither the old nor the new. It was a kind of emotional wilderness, a time when it wasn't quite clear who you were or what was real.

It is important for people to understand and not be surprised by this neutral zone, for several reasons. First, if you don't understand and expect it, you're more likely to try to rush through or even bypass the neutral zone—and to be discouraged when you find that doesn't work. You may mistakenly conclude that the confusion you feel there is a sign that something is wrong with you.

Second, you may be frightened in this no-man's-land and try to escape. (Employees do this frequently, which is why there is often an increased level of turnover during organizational changes.) To abandon the situation, however, is to abort the transition, both personally and organizationally—and to jeopardize the change.

Third, if you escape prematurely from the neutral zone, you'll not only compromise the change but also lose a great opportunity. Painful though it is, the neutral zone is the individual's and the organization's best chance to be creative, to develop into what they need to become, and to renew themselves. The positive function of the neutral zone will be discussed further in a later chapter, so here let me simply say that the gap between the old and the new is the time when innovation is most possible and when the organization can most easily be revitalized.

The neutral zone is thus both a dangerous and an opportune place, and it is the very core of the transition process. It is the time when repatterning takes place: old and maladaptive habits are replaced with new ones that are better adapted to the world in which the organization now finds itself. It is the winter in which the roots begin to prepare themselves for spring's renewal. It is the night during which we are disengaged from yesterday's concerns and preparing for tomorrow's. It is the chaos into which the old form dissolves and from which the new form emerges. It is the seedbed of the new beginnings that you seek.

Ending—neutral zone—new beginning. You need all three phases, and in that order, for a transition to work. The phases don't happen separately; they often go on at the same time. Endings are going on in one place, in another everything is in neutral zone chaos, and in yet another place the new beginning is already palpable. Calling them "phases" makes it sound as though they are lined up like rooms in a house. Perhaps it would be more accurate to think of them as three *processes* and to say that the transition cannot be completed until all three have taken place.

Letting go, repatterning, and making a new beginning: together these processes reorient and renew people when things are changing all around them. You need the transition that they add up to for the change to get under the surface of things and affect how people actually work. Without them, there may be dust and noise, but when things quiet down and the dust settles, nothing is really different. Most organizations, however, pay no attention to endings, don't acknowledge the neutral zone (and try to avoid it), and do nothing to help people make a fresh, new beginning, even as they trumpet the changes. Then they wonder why their people have so much difficulty with change.

When I say that *organizations* do these things, I mean, of course, that people do. Only people—like you—can recognize that change works only if it

Faced with the choice between changing one's mind and proving that there is no need to do so, almost everybody gets busy on the proof.

JOHN KENNETH GALBRAITH,
AMERICAN ECONOMIST

He that will not apply new remedies must expect new evils.

FRANCIS BACON,
BRITISH PHILOSOPHER

is accompanied by transition. Only people—like you—can learn to manage transitions so that the changes that trigger them aren't jeopardized. Only people—like you—can implement change in such a way that people actually get through it and the organization doesn't end up being hurt rather than helped.

The following pages will show you how to do those things.[5]

1. See Paul Hochman, "The Brand Killer," *Forbes Small Business* (May 2002), pp. 59ff.

2. Quoted in "The Idea Generator," *HR Reporter* 5, no. 2 (February 1988), p. 3.

3. Such usage is not wrong, of course—just not helpful. In fact, "transition" is used in many settings to refer to drastic changes like losing your job. One company I worked with had a "transition section" on its intranet site that people went to when their job was being phased out. And outplacement firms talk about their work with "career transitions." Ugh!

4. "Ending," "letting go," and "loss" are related concepts that we'll be using more or less interchangeably. "Ending" refers to the thing that ceases. "Letting go" is what we have to do when that thing ceases. And "loss" is what we feel when we have to let go.

5. The appendixes provide more detailed information about managing transition. Appendix A is about assessing an organization's readiness for transition. (It helps to know what you are in for before you find yourself knee-deep in trouble.) Appendix B lays out a 10-step process for planning a transition. Appendices C, D, and E deal with the leader's role in getting an organization through transition, monitoring the transition process and finding out what trouble people may be having in it, and adjusting your career thinking and action to the reality of frequent change.

Chapter Two

A Test Case

We think in generalities, but we live in detail.
—ALFRED NORTH WHITEHEAD, BRITISH PHILOSOPHER

Chapter 1 was fairly theoretical. Unless you understand the basic transition model, you won't be able to use it. But only in actual situations can you use it, so let's look at a situation that I encountered in a software company. I was brought in because the service manager wanted to make some changes, and his staff was telling him it wasn't going to be as easy as he thought.

He told me that he didn't see why that should be so. The change made perfect sense, and it was also necessary for the firm's continued leadership in the field of business software for banks. "Besides," he said, "no one's going to lose a job or anything like that."

Bearing in mind what you read in chapter 1, see what you think.

The company's service unit did most of its business over the telephone. Individual technicians located in separate cubicles fielded callers' questions. The company culture was very individualistic. Not only were employees referred to as "individual contributors," but each was evaluated based on the number of calls he or she disposed of in a week. At the start of each year a career evaluation plan was put together for each employee in which a target (a little higher than the total of the previous year's weekly numbers) was set. To hit the target brought you a bonus. To miss it cost you that bonus.

Purchasers of the company's big, custom software packages called to report various kinds of operating difficulties, and the calls were handled by people in three different levels. First the calls went to relatively inexperienced individuals, who could answer basic questions. They took the calls on an availability basis. If the problem was too difficult for the first level, it went to the second tier. Technicians at that level had more training and experience and could field most of the calls, but if they couldn't take care of a problem, they passed it on to someone on the third level. The "thirds" were programmers who knew the system from the ground up and could, if necessary, tell the client how to reprogram the software to deal with the problem.

Each tier of the service unit was a skill-based group with its own manager, who was responsible for managing the workload and evaluating the performance of the individual contributors. Not surprisingly, there was some rivalry and mistrust among the different levels, as each felt that its task was the pivotal one and that the others didn't pull their weight.

As you may have surmised, there were several inherent difficulties with this system. First, customers never got the same person twice unless they remembered to ask. Worse yet, there was poor coordination among the three levels. A level-one technician never knew to whom he was referring a customer—or sometimes even whether anyone at the next level actually took over the customers when he passed them on. Customers were often angry at being passed around rather than being helped.

Managers were very turf-conscious, and this didn't improve coordination. Sometimes the second-tier manager announced that all the "seconds" were busy—although this was hard to ascertain because each technician was hidden in a cubicle—and then the service would go on hold for a day (or even a week) while the seconds caught up with their workload. In the meantime, the frustrated customer might have called back and found that he had to start over again and explain the problem to a different first-tier worker.

Not only were customers passed along from one part of the service unit to another, but sometimes they were "mislaid" entirely. The mediocre (at best) level of customer satisfaction hadn't been as damaging when the company had no real competition, but when another company launched an excellent new product earlier that year, it spelled trouble.

The general manager of the service unit brought in a service consultant, who studied the situation and recommended that the unit be reorganized into teams of people drawn from all three of the levels. (This reorganization is what in the last chapter I called the *change*.) A customer would be assigned to a team, and the team would have the collective responsibility of solving the customer's problem. Each team would have a coordinator responsible for steering the customer through the system of resources. Everyone agreed: the change ought to solve the problem.

The change was explained at a unitwide meeting, where large organization charts and team diagrams lined the walls. Policy manuals were rewritten, and the team coordinators—some of whom had been level managers and some of whom were former programmers—went through a two-day training seminar. The date for the reorganization was announced, and each team met with the general manager, who told them how important the change was and how important their part was in making it work.

Although there were problems when the reorganization occurred, no one worried too much, because there are always problems with change. But a month or so later it became clear that the new system not only wasn't working but didn't even exist except on paper. The old levels were still entrenched in everyone's mind, and customers were still being tossed back and forth (and often dropped) without any system of coordination. The coordinators maintained their old ties with people from their former groups and tended to try to get things done with the help of their old people (even when those people belonged to another team) rather than by their team as a whole.

Imagine that you're brought in to help them straighten out this tangle. What would you do? Because we can't discuss the possibilities face to face, I will give you a list of actions that might be taken in such a situation. Scan them and see which sound like good ideas to you. Then go back through the list slowly and put a number by each item, assigning it to one of the following five categories:

1 = Very important. Do this at once.

2 = Worth doing but takes more time. Start planning it.

3 = Yes and no. Depends on how it's done.

4 = Not very important. May even be a waste of effort.

5 = No! Don't do this.

Fill in those numbers before you read further, and take your time. This is not a simple situation, and solving it is a complicated undertaking.

Possible Actions to Take

_____ Explain the changes again in a carefully written memo.

_____ Figure out exactly how individuals' behavior and attitudes will have to change to make teams work.

_____ Analyze who stands to lose something under the new system.

_____ Redo the compensation system to reward compliance with the changes.

_____ "Sell" the problem that is the reason for the change.

_____ Bring in a motivational speaker to give employees a powerful talk about teamwork.

_____ Design temporary systems to contain the confusion during the cutover from the old way to the new.

_____ Use the interim between the old system and the new to improve the way in which services are delivered by the unit—and, where appropriate, create new services.

_____ Change the spatial arrangements so that the cubicles are separated only by glass or low partitions.

_____ Put team members in contact with disgruntled clients, either by phone or in person. Let them see the problem firsthand.

_____ Appoint a "change manager" to be responsible for seeing that the changes go smoothly.

_____ Give everyone a badge with a new "teamwork" logo on it.

_____ Break the change into smaller stages. Combine the firsts and seconds, then add the thirds later. Change the managers into coordinators last.

_____ Talk to individuals. Ask what kinds of problems they have with "teaming."

_____ Change the spatial arrangements from individual cubicles to group spaces.

_____ Pull the best people in the unit together as a model team to show everyone else how to do it.

_____ Give everyone a training seminar on how to work as a team.

_____ Reorganize the general manager's staff as a team and reconceive the GM's job as that of a coordinator.

_____ Send team representatives to visit other organizations where service teams operate successfully.

_____ Turn the whole thing over to the individual contributors as a group and ask them to come up with a plan to change over to teams.

_____ Scrap the plan and find one that is less disruptive. If that one doesn't work, try another. Even if it takes a dozen plans, don't give up.

_____ Tell them to stop dragging their feet or they'll face disciplinary action.

_____ Give bonuses to the first team to process 100 client calls in the new way.

_____ Give everyone a copy of the new organization chart.

_____ Start holding regular team meetings.

_____ Change the annual individual targets to team targets, and adjust bonuses to reward team performance.

_____ Talk about transition and what it does to people. Give coordinators a seminar on how to manage people in transition.

There are no correct answers in this list, but over time I've come to trust some interventions more than others. Let me offer my own lists—with the acknowledgment that you really have to know more than I have told you to be sure of your vote. Your logic is more important than your vote, so I have included mine in comments on each item.

Category 1: Very important. Do this at once.
Figure out exactly how individuals' behavior and attitudes will have to change to make teams work.   To deal successfully with *transition,* you need to determine precisely what changes in their existing behavior and attitudes people will have to make. It isn't enough to tell them that they have to work as a team. They need to know how teamwork differs behaviorally and attitudinally from the way they are working now. What must they stop doing, and what are they going to have to start doing? Be specific. Until these changes are spelled out, people won't be able to understand what you tell them.

Analyze who stands to lose something under the new system.   This step follows the previous one. Remember, transition starts with an ending. You can't grasp the new thing until you've let go of the old thing. It's this process of letting go that people resist, not the change itself. Their resistance can take the form of foot-dragging or sabotage, and you have to understand the pattern of loss to be ready to deal with the resistance and keep it from getting out of hand.

"Sell" the problem that is the reason for the change.   Most managers and leaders put 10% of their energy into selling the problem and 90% into selling the solution to the problem. People aren't in the market for solutions to problems they don't see, acknowledge, and understand. They might even come up with a better solution than yours, and then you won't have to sell it—it will be theirs.

Put team members in contact with disgruntled clients, either by phone or in person. Let them see the problem firsthand.   This is part of selling the problem. As long as you are the only one fielding complaints, poor service is going to be *your* problem, no matter how much you try to get your subordinates to acknowledge its importance. To engage their energies, you must make poor service *their* problem. Client visits are the best opportunity for people to see how their operation is perceived by its customers. DuPont has used this program very successfully in a number of its plants. Under its "Adopt a Customer" program, blue-collar workers are sent to visit customers once a month and bring what they learn back to the factory floor.

Talk to individuals. Ask what kinds of problems they have with "teaming." When an organization is having trouble with change, managers usually say they know what is wrong. But the truth is that often they don't. They imagine that everyone sees things as they do, or they make assumptions about others that are untrue. You need to ask the right questions. If you ask, "Why aren't you doing this?" you've set up an adversarial relation and will probably get a defensive answer. If, on the other hand, you ask, "What problems are you having with this?" you're likelier to learn why it isn't happening.

Talk about transition and what it does to people. Give coordinators a seminar on how to manage people in transition.   Everyone can benefit from understanding transition. A coordinator will deal with subordinates better if he or she understands what they are going through. If they understand what transition feels like, team members will feel more confident that they haven't taken a wrong turn. They'll also see that some of their problems come from the transition process and not from the details of the change. If they don't understand transition, they'll blame the change for what they are feeling.

Start holding regular team meetings.   Even before you can change the space to fit the new teams, you can start building the new identity by having those groups meet regularly. In this particular organization, the plan had been to hold meetings every two weeks. We changed that immediately: the teams met every morning for ten minutes for the first two months. Only such frequent clustering can override the old habits and the old self-images and build the new relations that teamwork requires. And you can give no stronger message about a new priority than to give it a visible place on everyone's calendar.

Category 2: Worth doing but takes more time. Start planning it.

Redo the compensation system to reward compliance with the changes. This is important because you need to stop rewarding the old behavior. But do it carefully. A reward system that comes off the top of someone's head is likely to introduce new problems faster than it clears up old ones.

Design temporary systems to contain the confusion during the cutover from the old way to the new.   The time between the end of old ways and the beginning of new ones is a dangerous period. Things fall through the cracks. You'll learn more about this when we talk about the neutral zone, but for now, suffice to say that you may have to create temporary policies, procedures, reporting relationships, roles, and even technologies to get you through this chaotic time.

Use the interim between the old system and the new to improve the ways in which services are delivered by the unit—and, where appropriate, create new services.   This is the flip side of the chaotic "in-between" time: when everything is up for grabs anyway, innovations can be introduced more easily than during stable times. It's a time to try doing things in new ways—especially new ways that people have long wanted to try but that conflicted with the old ways.

Change the spatial arrangements from individual cubicles to group spaces. Until this is done, the new human configuration has no connection with the physical reality of the place. Space is symbolic. If they're all together physically, people are more likely to feel together mentally and emotionally.

Reorganize the general manager's staff as a team and reconceive the GM's job as that of a coordinator.   Leaders send many more messages than they realize or intend to. Unless the leader is modeling the behavior that he or she is seeking to develop in others, things aren't likely to change very much. As Ralph Waldo Emerson said, "What you are speaks so loudly I can't hear what you say."

Send team representatives to visit other organizations where service teams operate successfully.   People need to see, hear, and touch to learn effectively. Talking to someone who's actually doing something carries more weight with a doubtful person than even the best seminar or the most impressive pep talk. If you can't take people to another location, invite a representative to your location and get a videotape that shows how work is done there.

Change the annual individual targets to team targets, and adjust bonuses to reward team performance.   It's hard to get people who are used to going it alone to play on a team, and you'll never succeed until the game is redefined as a team sport. Annual performance schedules are part of what defines the game. Make this important change as soon as you can.

Category 3: Yes and no. Depends on how it's done.

Bring in a motivational speaker to give employees a powerful talk about teamwork.   The problem is that, by itself, this solution accomplishes nothing. And too often it *is* done by itself, as though, once "motivated," people will make the change they are supposed to. This method should be integrated into a comprehensive transition management plan to be effective.

Appoint a "change manager" to be responsible for seeing that the changes go smoothly.   This is a good idea if you have a well-planned undertaking, complete with communication, training, and support. But if you merely appoint someone and say, "Make it happen," you are unlikely to accomplish anything. If the person isn't very skilled, he or she may become simply an enforcer and weaken the change effort.

Give everyone a badge with a new "teamwork" logo on it.   Symbols are great, and you should use them, but most badges are meaningless bits of tinsel. They have to be part of a larger, comprehensive effort. (A lot of issues come back to that point, and so will we.)

Give everyone a training seminar on how to work as a team.   Seminars are important because people have to learn the new way. But much training is wasted because it's not part of a larger, comprehensive effort.

Change the spatial arrangements so that the cubicles are separated only by glass or low partitions.   You're on the right track—individual cubicles *do* reinforce the old behavior—but this solution doesn't go far enough because it doesn't use space creatively to reinforce the new identity as "part of a team." See Category 2 for a better solution.

Give bonuses to the first team to process 100 client calls in the new way. Rewards and competition can both serve your effort, but be sure not to set simplistic quantitative goals. Those 100 clients can be "processed" in ways that send them right out the door and into the competition's arms. In addition, speed can be achieved by a few team members doing all the work. You want to reward *teamwork,* so plan your competition carefully.

Category 4: Not very important. May even be a waste of effort.
Explain the changes again in a carefully written memo.   When you put things in writing, people can't claim later that they weren't told. Memos are actually better ways of protecting the sender, however, than they are of informing the receiver. And they are especially poor as ways to convey complex information—like how a reorganization is going to be undertaken.

Give everyone a copy of the new organization chart.   An organization chart can help to clarify complex groupings and reporting relationships, but this solution is pretty straightforward. It's the new attitudes and behavior we're concerned with here, not which VP people report to.

Category 5: No! Don't do this.
Turn the whole thing over to the individual contributors as a group and ask them to come up with a plan to change over to teams.   Involvement is fine, but it has to be carefully prepared and framed within realistic constraints. Simply to turn the power over to people who don't want a change to happen is to invite catastrophe.

Break the change into smaller stages. Combine the firsts and seconds, then add the thirds later. Change the managers into coordinators last.   This one is tempting because small changes are easier to assimilate than big ones. But one change after another is trouble. It's better to introduce change in one coherent package.

Pull the best people in the unit together as a model team to show everyone else how to do it.   This is even more appealing, but it strips the best people out of the other units and hamstrings the other groups' ability to duplicate the model team's accomplishments.

Scrap the plan and find one that is less disruptive. If that one doesn't work, try another. Even if it takes a dozen plans, don't give up.   If there is one thing that is harder than a difficult transition, it is a whole string of them occurring because somebody is pushing one change after another and forgetting about transition.

Tell them to stop dragging their feet or they'll face disciplinary action. Don't make threats. They build ill will faster than they generate positive results. But do make expectations clear. People who don't live up to them will have to face the music.

As you look back over my comments and compare them to your own thinking, reflect on the *change-transition* difference again. When people come up with very different answers than I have offered, it is usually because they forgot that it was transition and not change that they were supposed to be watching out for. Change needs to be managed too, of course. But it won't do much good to get everyone into the new teams and the new seating arrangements if all of the old behavior and thinking continue. As you read the rest of the book, keep reminding yourself that it isn't enough to change the situation. You also have to help people make the psychological reorientation that they must make if the change is to work. The following chapters provide dozens of tactics that have proved helpful in doing that.

In chapter 8 you'll find another case and another chance to try your hand at a transition management plan. But first let's look at some well-tested transition management tactics. Chapters 3, 4, and 5 deal with how to manage, respectively, endings, neutral zones, and new beginnings. Managing nonstop change is the subject of chapter 6, and chapter 7 provides ways to manage your own situation better. When you reach the next case study, you'll be full of ideas.

Part TWO

The Solutions

Chapter Three

How to Get People to Let Go

Every beginning is a consequence. Every beginning ends something.
—Paul Valéry, French poet

Almost anything is easier to get into than out of.
—Agnes Allen, American writer

Before you can begin something new, you have to end what used to be. Before you can learn a new way of doing things, you have to unlearn the old way. Before you can become a different kind of person, you must let go of your old identity. So beginnings depend on endings. The problem is, people don't like endings.

Yet change and endings go hand in hand: change causes transition, and transition starts with an ending. If things change within an organization, at least some of the employees and managers are going to have to let go of something. Here are some examples:

1. A hospital administrator decides to consolidate maternal and pediatric services. The reorganization makes terrific sense from the patient's point of view—and customer service is the name of the game these days! It will also save overhead costs, and cost-cutting is just as important today. So the idea is a real winner. But right now there are two completely different organizations, two different patterns of loyalty, two different career paths, two different sets of procedures. There are even two organizational cultures—one developed from working with adults and one developed from working with children. Each of these differences is a part of unit members' separate identities. People in both units talk about "us" and "them." People will have to let go of a whole world of doing and thinking to make the new arrangement work.

2. The newly appointed controller of a large corporation decides to reorganize the archaic and inefficient way in which financial transactions are handled. The old work flow has been a "bucket brigade": the whole line works only as fast as its slowest bucket-handler, and an embarrassingly large amount of data gets "spilled" along the way. So he redesigns the work flow, and to make the new process work he redesigns the organizational chart. Formerly separate functions are combined, and formerly joined functions are separated. People have new bosses, and the bosses have new responsibilities. Managers depend on the cooperation of people they don't know well, and they miss their buddies who used to help them get the job done in the old way. But the new system will work like a charm—he keeps saying.

3. A new general manager arrives at a manufacturing plant and finds that there are eight layers of supervision and management between him and the hourly workers. Information takes forever to move up or down the line, and when it arrives, it is often distorted. Decisions take months as problems are bumped up a level at a time until finally someone acts. Then implementation takes forever as it filters down level by level. "Too many managers," he announces. "We're going to trim the workforce and flatten the pyramid." Of the 60 managers and supervisors, 17 are close to retirement anyway, so they are lured out the door with sweetened retirement benefits. Six others are poor performers and are simply laid off, and 10 more are "reassigned"—which means "demoted," although no one will admit that. "There," says the GM. "Now we're trim and efficient." But as months go by the results get worse and worse. People are dragging their feet. Rumors abound. The GM keeps talking about how much better the new structure is than the old, hoping that somehow he can convince people to make it work. In logical terms it is better, but he doesn't realize that his words sound hollow to people who have lost their familiar turf, their sense of self-worth, and many of their good friends.

It isn't the *changes* themselves that the people in these cases resist. It's the losses and endings that they have experienced and the *transition* that they are resisting. That's why it does little good for you to talk about how healthy the outcome of a change will be. Instead, you have to deal directly with the losses and endings.

But how do you do that? Here's how.

Identify Who's Losing What

What is actually ending, and who is losing what? If you're in the planning stage, these questions can be answered in the following sequence:

1. *Describe the change in as much detail as you can.* What is actually going to change? Be specific. Terms like "improved quality," "decentralized decisionmaking," and "lower costs" don't tell people what is going to be different when the dust clears.

2. Imagine that the change is a cue ball rolling across the surface of a pool table. There are lots of other balls on the table, and it's going to hit a few of them—some because you planned it that way and some unintentionally. Try to foresee as many of those hits as you can. *What are the secondary changes that your change will probably cause? And what are the further changes that those secondary changes will cause?* As in the first step, describe exactly what will be different when each of those changes is completed.

3. You have now started a chain of cause-and-effect collisions. Think of the people whose familiar way of being and doing will be affected. In each case, *who is going to have to let go of something?* What exactly must they let go of? Is it their peer group? Is it the roles that gave them a sense of competence? Is it their chances for promotion? Is it the strategies that fit with their values? Is it their old expectations?

4. Notice that many of these losses aren't concrete. They are part of the inner complex of attitudes and assumptions and expectations that we all carry around in our heads. These inner elements of "the way things are" are what make us feel at home in our world. When they disappear, we've lost something very important, although to someone else it may seem as though nothing has changed.

5. Beyond these specific losses, *is there something that is over for everyone?* Is it a chapter in the organization's history? Is it an unspoken assumption about what the employees can expect from their employer? Is it something that the organization stands for? Whatever has ended might be described with a phrase like one of these:

   "We take care of our people."

"We are a cutting-edge high-tech company."

"We won't settle for finishing second."

"We won't be undersold."

"We will always act ethically."

"We promote from within."

If, on the other hand, the change is already under way, you can find out about losses much more quickly. Simply ask people. "What's different, now that we have a new X?" "When we did X, what did you have to give up?" "What do you miss since we changed X?"

Accept the Reality and Importance of the Subjective Losses

We have come out of the time when obedience, the acceptance of discipline, intelligent courage, and resolution were most important, into that more difficult time when it is a person's duty to understand the world rather than simply fight for it.

ERNEST HEMINGWAY,
AMERICAN WRITER

Don't argue with what you hear. In the first place, it will stop the conversation and you won't learn any more. In the second place, loss is a subjective experience, and your "objective" view (which is really just another subjective view) is irrelevant. Finally, you'll just make your task more difficult by convincing people that you don't understand them—or, worse yet, that you don't care what they feel and think.

Maybe you *don't* care. Maybe in the old days when you first started managing people, you learned to give orders and to crack the whip if they weren't carried out. Compliance was enough in those days because there wasn't so much competition and it took only half of people's energy and intelligence to do a decent job. But today it's different. Mere compliance is nowhere near enough. You need everyone's commitment because only with commitment will you get people to give 100%. And you won't get people's commitment unless you understand them and make decisions based on that understanding. So however you do it, learn who is experiencing a loss of some kind and what it is they are losing.

Don't Be Surprised at Overreaction

People seem to "overreact" to a change when they are reacting more than we are. But when we think that way, we overlook two things: first, that changes cause transitions, which cause losses, and it is the losses, not the changes, that they're reacting to; and second, that it's a piece of *their* world that is being lost, not a piece of ours, and we often react that way ourselves when it's part of our own world that is being lost. Being reasonable is much easier if you have little or nothing at stake.

"Overreaction" also comes from the experience that people have had with loss in the past. When old losses haven't been adequately dealt with, a sort of *transition deficit* is created—a readiness to grieve that needs only a new ending to set it off. We see this when people overreact to the dismissal of an obviously ineffective manager or leader or to some apparently insignificant change in policy or procedure. What they are actually reacting to is one or more losses in the past that have occurred without any acknowledgment or chance to grieve.

This same kind of overreaction occurs when an ending is viewed as symbolic of some larger loss. The minor layoff in a company that has never had layoffs before is an example. It isn't the loss of the particular individuals—it's the loss of the safety people felt from the no-layoff policy.

Overreactions also take place when a small loss is perceived as the first step in a process that might end with removing the grievers themselves. Someone whose job seemed secure is dismissed, and 100 coworkers begin to wonder, *Am I next?*

In all of these cases, overreaction is normal and not really overreaction at all. Learn to look for the loss behind the loss and deal with that underlying issue. You'll get much further if you can show people that Loss A is really unrelated to the dreaded, larger Loss B than if you simply try to talk them out of their reaction to Loss A.

Acknowledge the Losses Openly and Sympathetically

You need to bring losses out into the open—acknowledge them and express your concern for the affected people. Do it simply and directly:

> "I'm sorry that we're having to make these transfers. I know that we're losing good people."

> "I know that switching to the new software is going to leave a lot of you feeling like beginners again. I feel that way myself, and I hate it!"

> "Hey, Charlie, I heard that you got the pink slip. That's really tough! I wish they could have figured some way around that."

I know that most men, including those at ease with problems of the greatest complexity, can seldom accept even the simplest and most obvious truth if it be such as would oblige them to admit the falsity of conclusions which they have delighted in explaining to colleagues, which they have proudly taught to others, and which they have woven, thread by thread, into the fabric of their lives.

LEO TOLSTOY,
RUSSIAN WRITER

Managers are sometimes worried about talking so openly, some even arguing that it will "stir up trouble" to acknowledge people's feelings. What such an argument misses is that it is not talking about a loss but rather pretending that it doesn't exist that stirs up trouble.

An electronics company had to lay off several dozen longtime employees, and fairly attractive severance packages were put together to reward them for their loyal service. It happened that these workers had to stay at their jobs for two months after the announcement was made, and their manager explained that he wasn't going to talk to them explicitly about their loss, "because calling attention to it will just make them feel worse." His silence made them feel so angry that several of them began plotting ways to sabotage his unit's key project.

What that manager was really saying was that he didn't know how to handle the pain his employees felt. Many people find it difficult to deal openly with others' pain. But the research on what helps people recover from loss agrees that they recover more quickly if the losses can be openly discussed.

I saw this point demonstrated some time ago in a factory that had been targeted for closure. I watched a crowd of upset employees, who were listening to the executive who'd been sent out to explain the decision, relax and drop their belligerent manner when the executive interrupted his explanation to express his personal distress at having to close the plant. The man later apologized to several of us for the "display of emotion," not realizing that his honest feeling won the employees over more than his logical explanation.

Expect and Accept the Signs of Grieving

When endings take place, people get angry, sad, frightened, depressed, and confused. These emotional states can be mistaken for bad morale, but they aren't. They are the *signs of grieving,* the natural sequence of emotions people go through when they lose something that matters to them. You find these emotions in families that have lost a member, and you find them in an organization where an ending has taken place.[1]

Yet those emotions may not be evident, especially at first. People may deny that the loss will take place. *Denial* is a natural first stage in the grieving process, a way in which hurt people protect themselves from the first impact of loss. It is healthy and doesn't demand action on your part if it doesn't last very long. But if your people stay in denial for more than a few days after the handwriting is legible on the wall, you're going to need to address the issue. You may want to say something like this: "A lot of you are acting as though X isn't for real. Well, it is. Your actions concern me because I want all of us to get through this change with as little distress and disruption as possible. We'll never do that if we pretend it isn't happening."

As for the rest of the emotions grieving people feel, treat them seriously, but don't consider them as something you personally caused. Don't get defensive or argue. Here are some of those emotions and what you can do to deal with them successfully.

Anger: everything from grumbling to rage, often misdirected or undirected. Anger can lead to foot-dragging, "mistakes," and even sabotage. Listen . . . acknowledge that the anger is understandable. Don't take on the blame if it is being misdirected toward you. Distinguish between the acceptable feelings and unacceptable acting-out behavior: "I understand how you feel, but I'm not going to let you mess up the project."

Bargaining: unrealistic attempts to get out of the situation or to make it go away. People may try to strike a special deal or make big promises that they'll "save you a bundle of money" or "double the output" if you'll only undo the change. Distinguish these efforts from real problem-solving, keep a realistic outlook, and don't be swayed by desperate arguments and impossible promises.

Anxiety: silent or expressed, a realistic fear of an unknown and probably difficult future or simply catastrophic fantasies. Anxiety is natural, so don't make people feel stupid for feeling it. Just keep feeding them the information as it comes and commiserate with them when it doesn't.

Sadness: expressed with everything from silence to tears—the heart of the grieving process. Encourage people to say what they are feeling, and share your feelings too. Don't try to reassure people with unrealistic suggestions of hope, and don't feel that you have to make the feelings go away. Sympathize.

Disorientation: confusion and forgetfulness even among well-organized people; feelings of being lost and insecure. Give people extra support—opportunities to get things off their chests, reassurances that disorientation is natural and that other people feel it too. And give them extra attention.

Depression: feelings of being down, flat, dead; feelings of hopelessness; being tired all the time. Like sadness and anger, depression is hard to be around. You can't make it go away, however. People have to go through it, not around it. Make it clear that you understand and even share the feeling yourself, but that work still needs to be done. Do whatever you can to restore people's sense of having some control over their situation.

Not everyone feels all of these feelings intensely, and people don't go through them by the numbers. But within any group you can expect to encounter all of them, and you need to get people to recognize that they can accept the situation and move forward if they work through these emotions. The danger is not from these emotions themselves, but rather from the way they make people afraid of what is happening to them.

If you suppress the feelings and push people to get over them, you'll be handicapped with people who never "mended." In my work I have seen teams, departments, and sometimes entire companies fall apart because they never found a way to grieve over a significant loss.

Compensate for the Losses

"No pain, no gain," they say. But many change efforts fail because the people affected experience only the pain. The company may gain, but for employees it seems to be all loss. Trying to talk them out of their feelings will get you nowhere. Find a way to act. Here are some examples:

1. A large financial services company reorganized its clerical force and retrained the clerks to do what the lead clerks and the supervisors had formerly done. These latter folks were going to be mere clerks under the new system, and they did everything they could to badmouth and undermine the new plans. Then the manager had an idea. She brought them together as a "training task force" to create a program—not only to bring their former subordinates up to speed but also to train new hires. Although these "demoted" people lost hierarchical status, they were given new status as technical experts and trainers, and they kept the new roles even after the change was accomplished. Their opposition turned slowly into cooperation and support.

2. The U.S. Forest Service went through funding cutbacks in the early 1980s. As the logging industry declined, so did the need for the timber specialists who had been the backbone of the service. At the same time, recreation gained more prominence, as did ecology, public information, computer services, and wildlife biology. The old-line foresters lost promotions, power, even jobs. So, following the principle of giving back in one area what has been lost in another, the Forest Service instituted career renewal programs to help people reorient their careers to the areas where opportunity was increasing. They even helped people plan new careers outside the Forest Service. People still felt their losses, but they moved through the grieving process and quickly became productive again.

3. A large state university reassigned one of its vice presidents to a far less important area than the one he had previously headed, and although no one called it a demotion, it was hard to see it as anything else. Everyone knew that he had been ineffective in his previous job, and his new job actually fit his talents far better, but he was deeply hurt by the move. Discussing the situation, we discovered that the man was less troubled by the fact of the move than by how he thought it would be perceived by his colleagues. Understanding the VP's real interests in the matter, the president was able to negotiate how the announcement was made and the decision explained. A crippling loss was turned into a temporary hurt, and a solid (if overpromoted) employee was saved.

The question to ask yourself is: *What can I give back to balance what's been taken away?* Status, turf, team membership, recognition? If people feel that the change has robbed them of control over their futures, can you find some way to give them back a feeling of control? If their feeling of competence has been taken away because their job disappeared, can you give them new feelings of competence in other functions with timely training?

This principle of compensating for losses is basic to all kinds of change, and even the most important or beneficial changes often fail because this principle is overlooked. As the journalist Walter Lippmann said 50 years ago: "Unless the reformer can invent something which substitutes attractive virtues for attractive vices, he will fail." Remember Lippmann's advice when you try to get people to accept programs in quality improvement or customer service, when you try to set up self-managed teams or introduce unfamiliar equipment, or when you flatten the organization or cut overhead.

Every exit is an entry somewhere else.

Tom Stoppard,
British dramatist

Give People Information, and Do It Again and Again

There are lots of rationalizations for not communicating. Here are some common ones:

"They don't need to know yet. We'll tell them when the time comes. It'll just upset them now." For every week of upset that you avoid by hiding the truth, you gain a month of bitterness and mistrust. Besides, the grapevine already has the news, so don't imagine that your information is a secret.

"They already know. We announced it." Okay, you told them, but it didn't sink in. Threatening information is absorbed remarkably slowly. Say it again. And find different ways to say it and different media (large meetings, one-on-ones, memos, a story in the company paper) in which to say it.

"I told the supervisors. It's their job to tell the rank and file." The supervisors are likely to be in transition themselves, and they may not even sufficiently understand the information to convey it accurately. Maybe they're still in denial. Information is power, so they may not want to share it yet. Don't assume that information trickles down through the organizational strata reliably or in a timely fashion.

"We don't know all the details yet ourselves, so there's no point in saying anything until everything has been decided." In the meantime, people can get more and more frightened and resentful. Much better to say what you do know, say that you don't know more, and provide a timetable for additional information. If information isn't available later when it was promised, don't forget to say something to show that you haven't forgotten your promise.

Those who honestly mean to be true contradict themselves more rarely than those who try to be consistent.

OLIVER WENDELL HOLMES
JR., AMERICAN JURIST

Of course, there may be times when information must be withheld temporarily. The Securities and Exchange Commission (SEC) may require it, for example, or you may not be able to talk about a strategic move because competitors will learn of it. But most of the time information is withheld because leaders or managers are uncomfortable giving it. That discomfort often arises not from the anticipated long-term effects but simply from the short-term impact—the setting off of the "grieving" emotions discussed earlier.

So instead of telling the truth, managers substitute a fabrication of half-truths and untruths. Not only do these later turn out to be outright lies, but managers often trip themselves up with inconsistencies and new stories to cover the old inconsistencies.

Define What's Over and What Isn't

One of the biggest problems that endings cause in an organization is confusion. Things change, and obviously the organization won't do some of the things it used to do. But which things? The boss says, "From here on, we're lean and mean!" Does that mean that we order 30% fewer supplies, or that we don't sweat the little stuff anymore, or that we have to give up the prospect of 40-hour weeks? The boss says, "We're really going to be customer-minded from now on." Does that mean that from now on we do everything the customer says? What about company policy and standard procedures—are they out the window? The boss says, "We're increasing spans of control by 50%." Does that mean that managers do all the old stuff faster or that they can let go of some of the old stuff?

One of the most important leadership roles during times of change is that of putting into words what it is time to leave behind. Because talking about making a break with the past can upset its defenders, some leaders shy away from articulating just what it is time to say good-bye to. But in their unwillingness to say what it is time to let go of, they are jeopardizing the very change that they believe they are leading.

Managers risk three equally serious and difficult reactions when they do not specify what is over and what isn't:

1. People don't dare to stop doing anything. They try to do all the old things *and* the new things. Soon they burn out with the overload.

2. People make their own decisions about what to discard and what to keep, and the result is inconsistency and chaos.

3. People toss out everything that was done in the past, and the baby disappears with the bathwater.

So think through each aspect of the changes you are making, and be specific about what goes and what stays. It takes time to do that, but undoing the damage wrought by any of these three reactions will take much longer.

Mark the Endings

Don't just talk about the endings—create actions or activities that dramatize them. When René McPherson took over the leadership of Dana Corporation, he found operations choked by a culture in which everything was covered by rules; though incredibly detailed, these rules nonetheless failed to cover all cases. Besides, no one could remember them all or even be sure in which of the company manuals a given rule could be found. McPherson wanted to change to a culture in which there were a few universally understood principles and in which the employees' intelligence and commitment were counted on to apply the principles wisely.

He explained all this, but when it came time to make the change, he chose action rather than words to convey his point. In a management meeting he piled all the company manuals on a table. They formed a stack almost two feet tall. Then he swept them onto the floor and held up a single sheet of paper on which the corporate principles were typed. "These are our new rules," he said.

If you want an even more dramatic action, think of the story that is told about the Spanish explorer Hernando Cortés. When he came ashore with his men at Veracruz, he knew they were extremely ambivalent about the task ahead of them. Some called it hopeless. Faced with a continent full of adversaries, everyone must have wished that he had never come. Cortés burned the ships.

A bit heavy-handed perhaps. Think back to the software company service unit I described in chapter 2. In changing from individual contributors to teams, they tore down the walls of the service technicians' cubicles and created work team spaces in which people could see and talk to their new collaborators. On a functional level the new space worked better. But just as important, the act of creating the new space sent a message: "The old way of separation is gone. We're doing things a new collaborative way now."

Treat the Past with Respect

Never denigrate the past. Many managers, in their enthusiasm for a future that is going to be better than the past, ridicule or talk slightingly of the old way of doing things. In doing so they consolidate the resistance against the transition because people identify with the way things used to be and thus feel that their self-worth is at stake whenever the past is attacked.

But managers who are tempted to denounce the past are not all wrong: they are right in wanting to distinguish what they are proposing from what has been tried in the past or what is being done in the present. The trick is to make the distinction nonjudgmentally. Here are some examples:

An executive is brought in to reorganize a division into business units. Rather than attacking the old functional organization as inefficient and archaic ("Nobody in his right mind would run a business *that* way!"), he credits it for bringing the organization to the point where it now stands: on the brink of an important development. He emphasizes the continuities he feels with his predecessor and talks about the new challenges that call for new responses.

The new director of a human resources department realizes that the compartmentalism of her group in the past led to conflicting policies and turf battles that made cooperation impossible. She avoids the devastating critique that she could deliver and instead sends key personnel out to visit customers—who deliver her critique for her. She then exposes key members of the old order to a couple of organizations where teamwork has greatly improved service and helps them formulate and spearhead plans for the change.

> *Historic continuity with the past is not a duty, it is only a necessity.*
> OLIVER WENDELL HOLMES, AMERICAN PHYSICIAN

Be careful that in urging people to turn away from the past you don't drive them away from you or from the new direction that the organization needs to take. Present innovations as developments that build on the past and help to realize its potential. Honor the past for what it has accomplished.

Let People Take a Piece of the Old Way with Them

Endings occur more easily if people can take a bit of the past with them. You are trying to disengage people from it, not stamp it out like an infection. And in particular, you don't want to make people feel blamed for having been part of it.

When Western Airlines was sold to Delta, the employee store at Los Angeles International Airport sold out of all items with the big red "W" company logo in a few hours. When the land occupied by Almaden Winery was sold to developers, employees lost one of the loveliest workplaces imaginable. They grieved especially for the winery rose garden, where people had strolled during breaks and spent lunch hours. Management discovered that the employees were going into the garden after work and taking rose cuttings to take home. Recognizing the significance of what was happening, management decided to help by providing the cuttings themselves.

Organizations can take even more initiative in tapping this longing for a piece of the past. A Procter & Gamble paper plant in northern Michigan put together a yearbook during the last year of the plant's operation. People brought in pictures, some twenty or thirty years old, and wrote little essays about the past. The "graduating class" of current workers was featured, along with such information as was available about where everyone was going after "graduation."

Show How Endings Ensure the Continuity of What Really Matters

A state without the means of some change is without the means of its conservation.

Edmund Burke, British statesman

Most endings are not so terminal as a plant closure or the sale of a company. In fact, many endings represent the only way to protect the continuity of something bigger. An out-of-date product line is discontinued and replaced so that a manufacturing company can keep its customers. Two hospitals merge (and lose their individual identities) because neither will be able to survive alone. The start-up company's seat-of-the-pants operating style, though exciting, is not adequate to manage the midsized company it has grown into. The old ways have to be relinquished before new systems will work. Again, people have to let go of a piece of their identity to protect the integrity of the whole.

Only the provisional endures.

French proverb

A corollary to this idea is that the past, which people are likely to idealize during an ending, was itself a time—and even *the product*—of change. When people start talking about "the good old days," it's easy to imagine that they are describing a peaceful time of stability. But that is selective memory. There were changes then too. Whenever something that is viewed as a break with the past turns out successfully, people forget the loss they felt when the change happened and begin to celebrate it as a "tradition." But the status quo is just an innovation brought about by a transition that people have forgotten.

Conservatism is the worship of dead revolutions.

Clinton Rossiter, American historian

Yesterday's ending launched today's success, and today will have to end if tomorrow's changes are to take place. Endings are not comfortable for any of us. But they are also neither unprecedented breaks with the past nor attempts by those in power to make people's lives miserable.

A Final Thought

With all of the foregoing emphasis on foreseeing and softening the painful effects of loss on employees, the reader might assume that I am urging that you slowly take things away a piece at a time. That would be a misreading of my advice, for the last thing an organization needs is too small an ending or an incomplete ending that requires a whole new round of losses to finish the job before the wounds from the old ones have healed. Whatever must end, *must end.* Don't drag it out. Plan it carefully, and once it is done, allow time for healing. But the action itself should be sufficiently large to get the job done.

In taking possession of a state, the conqueror should well reflect as to the harsh measures that may be necessary, and then execute them at a single blow. . . . Cruelties should be committed all at once.

NICCOLÒ MACHIAVELLI, ITALIAN POLITICAL PHILOSOPHER

Conclusion

The single biggest reason organizational changes fail is that no one has thought about endings or planned to manage their impact on people. Naturally concerned about the future, planners and implementers all too often forget that people have to let go of the present first. They forget that while the first task of *change management* is to understand the desired outcome and how to get there, the first task of *transition management* is to convince people to leave home. You'll save yourself a lot of grief if you remember that.

It doesn't work to leap a 20-foot chasm in two 10-foot jumps.

AMERICAN PROVERB

Managing Endings: A Checklist

Yes   No

____ ____   Have I studied the change carefully and identified who is likely to lose what—including what I myself am likely to lose?

____ ____   Do I understand the subjective realities of these losses to the people who experience them, even when they seem to me to be overreacting?

____ ____   Have I acknowledged these losses with sympathy?

____ ____   Have I permitted people to grieve and protected them from well-meant attempts to stop them from expressing their anger or sadness?

____ ____   Have I publicly expressed my own sense of loss, if I feel any?

____ ____   Have I found ways to compensate people for their losses?

___ ___ Am I giving people accurate information and doing it again and again?

___ ___ Have I defined clearly what is over and what isn't?

___ ___ Have I found ways to "mark the ending"?

___ ___ Am I being careful not to denigrate the past but, when possible, finding ways to honor it?

___ ___ Have I made a plan for giving people a piece of the past to take with them?

___ ___ Have I made it clear how the ending we are making is necessary to protect the continuity of the organization or conditions on which the organization depends?

___ ___ Is the ending we are making big enough to get the job done in one step?

Final Questions

What actions can you take to help people deal more successfully with the endings that are taking place in your organization? What can you do today to get started on this aspect of transition management? (Write yourself a memo in the space below.)

---

1. The stages of the grieving process were first described by Elisabeth Kübler Ross, M.D., in her now-classic book *On Death and Dying* (New York: Macmillan, 1969).

Chapter Four

Leading People Through the Neutral Zone

It's not so much that we're afraid of change or so in love with the old ways, but it's that place in between that we fear. . . . It's like being between trapezes. It's Linus when his blanket is in the dryer. There's nothing to hold on to.
　　—MARILYN FERGUSON, AMERICAN FUTURIST

One doesn't discover new lands without consenting to lose sight of the shore for a very long time.
　　—ANDRÉ GIDE, FRENCH NOVELIST

Just when you decide that the hardest part of managing transition is getting people to let go of the old ways, you enter a state of affairs in which neither the old ways nor the new ways work satisfactorily. People are caught between the demands of conflicting systems and end up immobilized, like Hamlet, trying to decide whether "to be or not to be." Or all systems break down and everyone enters what a client called a time of "radio silence."

If this phase lasted only a short time, you could just wait for it to pass. But when the change is deep and far-reaching, this time between the old identity and the new can stretch out for months, even years. And as Marilyn Ferguson so aptly put it, during this period after you've let go of the old trapeze, you feel as though you have nothing to hold on to while waiting for a new one to appear.

A Very Difficult Time . . .

To make matters worse, your boss is probably getting impatient. "How long is it going to take you to implement those changes?" she asks, and you can tell from the tone in her voice that she thinks it has already taken too long. You wish you could say something positive, but you realize you have to be careful about making promises. Frustration and tension are increasing, everyone seems to be moving at half speed, and you hear that some of the best people in the group have sent out their résumés.

Welcome to the middle phase of the transition process. This is a time most languages don't even have a name for. I call it the *neutral zone* because it is a nowhere between two somewheres, and because while you are in it, forward motion seems to stop while you hang suspended between *was* and *will be*.[1] Neutral zones occur not only in organizations but also in individual lives and in the history of whole societies. In the 1990s, for instance, the former Soviet Union struggled to emerge from the neutral zone that emerged after the collapse of the Communist system.

What the neutral zone is and why it exists can be seen in figure 4.1. It is a time when all the old clarities break down and everything is in flux. Things are up in the air. Nothing is a given anymore, and anything could happen. No one knows the answers: one person says one thing and someone else says something completely different.

The dangers presented by the neutral zone take several forms:

1. People's anxiety rises and their motivation falls. They feel disoriented and self-doubting. They are resentful and self-protective. Energy is drained away from work into coping tactics. In one recent merger, managers in several key departments of the smaller company estimated that people's effectiveness had fallen 50%.

2. People in the neutral zone miss more work than at other times. At best, productivity suffers, and at worst, there is a sharp rise in medical and disability claims. Absenteeism tripled at one bank that was cutting back its workforce. My firm had a terrible time scheduling transition management seminars there because some of the key managers were on medical leave.

3. Old weaknesses, previously patched over or compensated for, reemerge in full flower. If customer service has always been weak, it gets even worse in the neutral zone. That old resentment over the generous executive severance packages boils over, just when everyone's trust in the organization's leaders has been slipping anyway. And that problem with the communication (or supervision or public relations) that you thought was getting better suddenly gets very serious.

The crisis consists precisely in the fact that the old is dying and the new cannot be born. In this interregnum, a great variety of morbid symptoms appear.

ANTONIO GRAMSCI,
ITALIAN POLITICAL ACTIVIST

Illness strikes men when they are exposed to change.

HERODOTUS,
GREEK HISTORIAN

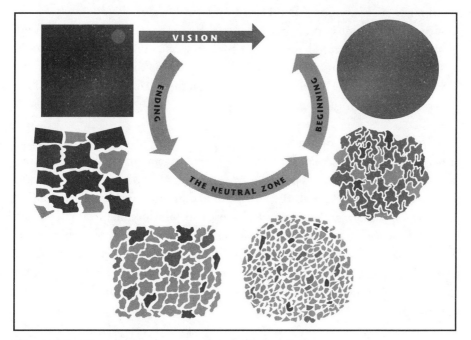

Figure 4.1 Transition: A square morphs into a circle.

4. In the neutral zone, people are overloaded, they frequently get mixed signals, and systems are in flux and therefore more than normally unreliable. It is only natural that priorities get confused, information is miscommunicated, and important tasks go undone. It is also natural that with so much uncertainty and frustration, people lose their confidence in the organization's future and turnover begins to rise. You could take your motto for neutral zone management from the caption of a Ziggy cartoon in which the little man sits in his car staring at a road sign reading, "Deep Doo-Doo, Next 750 Miles."

5. Given the ambiguities of the neutral zone, it is easy for people to become polarized: some want to rush forward and others want to go back to the old ways. Under the pressure of that polarization, consensus easily breaks down and the level of discord rises. Teamwork is undermined, as is loyalty to the organization itself. Managed properly, this is only a temporary situation. But left unmanaged, polarization can lead to terminal chaos. For this reason, some organizations never emerge from the neutral zone.

6. Finally, as Herodotus, the historian of a warlike age, would have pointed out, corporations and other organizations are vulnerable to attack from outside. Disorganized and tired, people respond slowly and halfheartedly to competitive threats. If they are resentful and looking for ways to pay the organization back, they may even sabotage the organization's ability to respond to the outside attacks.

It is for these reasons that managing the neutral zone is so essential during a period of enormous change. Neutral zone management isn't just something that would be nice if you had more time. It's the only way to ensure that the organization comes through the change intact and that the necessary changes actually work the way that they are supposed to. The argument that there isn't time for such efforts is based on a serious misunderstanding of the situation: neutral zone management actually *saves* time because you don't have to launch the change a second time . . . after the first time didn't work. And it's neutral zone management that prevents the organization from coming apart as it crosses the gap between the old way and the new.

. . . But Also a Creative Time

When everything is going smoothly, it's often hard to change things. "If it ain't broke," they say, "it don't need fixing." People who are sure they have the answers stop asking questions. And people who stop asking questions never challenge the status quo. Without such challenges, an organization can drift slowly into deep trouble before it gets a clear signal that something is wrong.

People from troubled organizations or outsiders who do not know much about the subject are often the ones who come up with the breakthrough answers. Such was the case with Henry Bessemer, the British inventor who perfected the process of making steel by decarbonizing iron with heated air. He knew very little about steelmaking, so (in his words) "I had an immense advantage over many others dealing with the problem. I had no fixed ideas derived from long-established practice to bias my mind, and did not suffer from the general belief that whatever is is right."[2]

Lacking clear systems and signals, the neutral zone is a chaotic time, but this lack is also the reason the neutral zone is more hospitable to new ideas than settled times. Because the neutral zone automatically puts people into Bessemer's situation, it is a time that is ripe with creative opportunity.

The task before you is therefore twofold: first, to get your people through this phase of transition in one piece; and second, to capitalize on all the confusion by encouraging them to be innovative. The road through the neutral zone is indeed rough going, but it is passable if you're prepared for it. Here's what to do to help people make the journey.

"Normalize" the Neutral Zone

One of the most difficult aspects of the neutral zone is that most people don't understand it. They expect to be able to move straight from the old to the new. But this isn't a trip from one side of the street to the other. It's a journey from one identity to another, and that kind of journey takes time.

The neutral zone is like the wilderness through which Moses led his people. That took 40 years, you remember—not because they were lost but because the generation that had known Egypt had to die off before the Israelites could enter the Promised Land. Taken literally, that's a pretty discouraging idea: that things won't really change until a whole generation of workers dies. But on a less literal level, the message of Moses's long journey through the wilderness is both less daunting and more applicable to your situation: the outlook, attitudes, values, self-images, and ways of thinking that were functional in the past have to "die" before people can be ready for life in the present. Moses took care of transition's ending phase when he led his people out of Egypt, but it was the 40 years in the neutral zone wilderness that *got Egypt out of his people.* It won't take you 40 years, but you aren't going to be able to do it in a few weeks either.

The neutral zone is not the wasted time of meaningless waiting and confusion that it sometimes seems to be. It is a time when reorientation and redefinition must take place, and people need to understand that. It is the winter during which the spring's new growth is taking shape under the earth.

People need to recognize that it is natural to feel somewhat frightened and confused at such a time. As the old patterns disappear from people's minds and the new ones begin to replace them, people can be full of self-doubts and misgivings about their leaders. As their ambivalence increases, so

Chaos often breeds life, while order breeds habit.

HENRY ADAMS,
AMERICAN HISTORIAN

It takes nine months to have a baby, no matter how many people you put on the job.

AMERICAN SAYING

Habit is habit, and not to be flung out of the window by any man, but coaxed downstairs a step at a time.

MARK TWAIN,
AMERICAN WRITER

Confusion is a word we have invented for an order which is not yet understood.

HENRY MILLER,
AMERICAN NOVELIST

does their longing for answers. That is why people in the neutral zone are so tempted to follow anyone who seems to know where he or she is going—including, unfortunately, troublemakers and people who are heading toward the exits. No wonder the neutral zone is a time when turnover increases. (Moses even had that problem himself, although in his day it was called worshiping strange gods.)

Redefine the Neutral Zone

Sometimes it's valuable to change the metaphor that people use to describe this uncomfortable time. In a manufacturing plant that was being closed, people were talking about the interim between the announcement and the closure as a time when "the ship was sinking." Needless to say, that metaphor encouraged them to get off the vessel as fast as they could, and the company—which was counting on the output of the plant until it actually closed—found itself facing the possibility that production at the facility would collapse before the company was ready for it to stop.

They needed a new metaphor that would have less disruptive implications for productivity. So they redefined the situation as the "last voyage" of the ship, a metaphor that accounted for the distress people were feeling but that emphasized the positive aspect of the situation. This last voyage was a time from which both the organization and the individuals could benefit. The organization needed the plant's output, and the individuals could use the time to improve their own marketability through skills enhancement, career-strategies training, and experience-building reassignments.

When, in the new metaphor, the ship "reached port," everyone could "disembark" in a planned fashion, better off for having stayed aboard and with the pride of a difficult job well done. As it turned out, the output of the plant recovered from its initial decline and within four months of the announcement began to rise. On a per-capita basis, the output almost doubled during the final months of the plant's operation. The "last voyage" of this group was an inspiring one, although the company mistakenly thought that it could cash in on it by extending the plant's life for a few more months. At that point, the people—whose earlier esprit de corps had been impressive—felt they were being jerked around, and productivity nosedived. Transition management must be based on win-win arrangements.

This talk about metaphors—about a "sinking ship" versus a "last voyage"—may seem like mere word-play. But the words are labels on two completely different ways of looking at a difficult situation. The new metaphor of a last voyage didn't invalidate the difficulty—that was a given. But it gave purpose to the situation, while the old metaphor left people feeling hopeless. The new metaphor carried the message "Make the most of this situation," while the old metaphor told people, "Get out of here as fast as you can."

But the leadership of the factory and the corporate division that was depending on its productivity did not merely talk in a new way. They put together new training programs and reassignment policies that translated the words into actions that people could see and profit from. They offered modest financial incentives for people to stay on board until their efforts were no longer needed, and they negotiated with other corporate units to hold positions open for those transferring until the factory was ready for them to go.

An adventure is only an inconvenience rightly understood. An inconvenience is only an adventure wrongly understood.

C. K. CHESTERTON,
BRITISH WRITER

Create Temporary Systems for the Neutral Zone

What can you do to give structure and strength during a time when people are likely to feel lost and confused?

1. You can try hard to protect people from further changes while they're trying to regain their balance. You won't always succeed, of course, because some new government regulation may send everyone back to square one, or some new product introduced by your main competitor may knock your sales for a loop. But many changes *can* be headed off or at least delayed. And if you cannot do so, you may be able to cluster the new change under a heading that makes it a part of a bigger change that you're going through. People can deal with a lot of change if it is coherent and part of a larger whole. But unrelated and unexpected changes, even small ones, can be the proverbial straw that breaks the camel's back.

2. Review policies and procedures to see that they are adequate to deal with the confusing fluidity of the neutral zone. The "rules" under which you operate were set up to govern ongoing operations when things weren't changing as much as they are now. Do you need a new policy to cover some aspect of the new situation—a policy, for instance, about job classifications,

priorities, time off for training, or who can make what kind of decision? Or do you need a new procedure for giving people temporary assignments, processing the work or handling overloads, identifying training needs, or scheduling meetings?

3. Consider a related question: What new roles, reporting relationships, or configurations of the organization chart do you need to develop to get through this time in the wilderness? Moses, with the help of Jethro (the first organizational development consultant in history), reorganized his decisionmaking process in the neutral zone by regrouping people into new units under new, temporary decisionmakers—"judges," in the parlance of his day. Hierarchy often breaks down in the neutral zone, and mixed groupings, like task forces and project teams, are often very effective. People may have to be given temporary titles or made "acting" managers.

4. You would do well to set short-range goals for people to aim toward and to establish checkpoints along the way toward longer-term outcomes that you are seeking. Now is a time when people get discouraged easily. It often seems that nothing important is happening in the neutral zone. So it is crucial to give people a sense of achievement and of movement, even if you have to stretch the point a bit. This helps to counter the feelings of being lost, of meaninglessness, and of self-doubt that are common in the neutral zone.

5. Don't set people up for failure by promising that you will deliver high levels of output while you are in the neutral zone. Everyone loses when such ambitious targets are missed: you look bad, people's self-confidence falls even further, and your superiors are upset. You may need to educate your superiors to get them to see that success at a lower level, which builds people up, is worth far more in the long run than failure at a higher level, which tears them down. Upper-level management hates to look bad, so help them to see the importance of setting realistic output objectives.

6. Find out what supervisors and managers need to learn to function successfully in the neutral zone and then provide special training programs in those subjects. These might include seminars on problem-solving, on team-building, and on transition management tactics.

Strengthen Intragroup Connections

The neutral zone is a lonely place. People feel isolated, especially if they don't understand what is happening to them. As I have already noted, old problems are likely to resurface and old resentments are likely to come back to life. For these reasons it is especially important to try to rebuild a sense of identification with the group and of connectedness with one another.

At a large aerospace facility that was being reorganized, connections were established through weekly meetings at which, over the course of a year, representatives from every group met with the general manager of the site for an informal meal. During the lunch the GM answered all questions and gathered suggestions for policy changes that would help people deal with being "in the wilderness." Week after week people returned to the project teams and departmental units with a new level of trust in and a greater feeling of connectedness with their leader.

At a food processing plant the leadership wanted a faster way to involve everyone, and so a Family Day was planned. The factory was shut down for a day, and everyone came together at a local theme park, where a large area had been rented for their gathering. Events were planned that not only mixed line workers with leaders and middle managers but blended groups that were becoming polarized under the confusions of the neutral zone. Managers worked hard to meet and reassure the families of the people who worked for them. The results were clear the very next morning—there was less anxiety and more solidarity between exempt and nonexempt workers, and within weeks productivity had improved measurably.

Communications help to keep people feeling included in and connected to the organization. Many companies have used newsletters, printed or online, as a way of maintaining contact with, and showing concern for, employees in the neutral zone. In the neutral zone there is often very little new information of the sort that produces public announcements and memos. Without a communication channel that is appropriate to a time of worry and waiting, rumors multiply and people alternate between anxiety and apathy.

In one corporation that was relocating its headquarters, the *Transition News* kept everyone abreast of progress, squelched rumors, and featured articles on schools, health care, shopping, real estate, and other aspects of the new location. A "Letters to the Editor" section answered questions.

At the Santa Clara, California, Intel fabricating plant, the newsletter explained the job posting system and described upcoming job search seminars. It also announced barbecues for several shifts and carried farewell messages from departing personnel.

At the Cheboygan, Michigan, Procter & Gamble paper products plant, a newsletter was used very effectively to maintain contact with employees during long months of uncertainty while the plant was being shut down. It included a folksy update on people who had found positions at other P&G plants, an advice column by the local employee assistance program specialist (who termed himself a "transition counselor"), news stories about the progress of the yearbook that was being created to record everyone's final year, and ads for the sale of cars, appliances, and prom dresses by families that were relocating.

In each case a newsletter was effectively used to keep in touch with people during a time when they tended to feel confused and disconnected. And not coincidentally, all three organizations made it through the neutral zone without the lasting damage that many organizations suffer there.

In the neutral zone, be wary of any arrangement or activity that shows a preference for one group over others. During this middle phase of transition, people want to feel that "we are all in this boat together"—another good metaphor. They will put up with a lot of discomfort if *everyone* must do so. But if there are people who, because of their position or connections, are getting special treatment, there will be trouble. That trouble can even be sparked by perquisites that individuals have always enjoyed. First-class air travel for upper-level managers, special parking spaces for staff members, and an executive dining room can all loom large as resentment-building symbols of privilege that send the unwitting message that some people have it easy during a difficult time when the rank and file is suffering.

Use a Transition Monitoring Team

One of the persistent problems during transition is the difficulty experienced by decisionmakers and those implementing decisions in remaining clear on the precise impact of the decisions and actions they've taken. Leaders usually assume that all the feedback they need will come up through regular channels and be voiced at staff meetings in reply to the question, "How are things going?" Such is seldom the case. As answers to that innocent question are filtered and interpreted and sometimes blocked on their way upward, they are inevitably distorted. Ed Carlson, the former CEO of United Airlines, used to call it the NETMA problem—Nobody Ever Tells Me Anything.

This is where a transition monitoring team is valuable. The TMT, as it is often called, is a group of seven to twelve people chosen from as wide a cross-section of the organization as possible. It meets every week or two to take the pulse of the organization in transition. It has no decisionmaking power and is not charged with suggesting courses of action. Rather, its purpose is to facilitate upward communication and to do three other things:

1. The very existence of the TMT demonstrates that the organization wants to know how things are going for people.

2. The TMT is an effective focus group to review plans or communications before they are announced. The leader may hear, "You'd better not say that. They'll think that you're going to . . . "

3. The TMT provides a point of ready access to the organization's grapevine and so can be used to correct misinformation and counter rumors.

Note a few warnings about using TMTs. First, make sure that the purpose of the group is clear. Don't leave the impression that it is a decision-making body or that it is "managing" the transition. It is simply monitoring it. Second, don't give the function to an existing group of upper-level managers; existing groups, with other responsibilities, have other agendas and won't give you the untainted reports that you need. Set up a special group, and make sure it represents different constituencies within the organization. Third, ensure that the TMT has access to the organization's leadership by including someone in the group who has the leader's ear. Fourth, make it clear that this is a time-limited group. Name a windup date at the start (although that can, of course, be changed), and help everyone understand that this is a task group required by the very important situation that the organization is in. Finally, don't let the concerns voiced by the group disappear: report back to the group regularly about what is being done about the issues it has raised, and be sure that at least some of their issues lead to visible actions.

Using the Neutral Zone Creatively

If you have always done it that way, it is probably wrong.

CHARLES KETTERING, AMERICAN INVENTOR

While it is essential to build into the neutral zone temporary systems for getting people through the wilderness intact, you need to do more. Capitalize on the break in normal routines that the neutral zone provides to do things differently and better. In the neutral zone the restraints on innovation are weakened. With everything up in the air anyway, people are more willing than usual to try new things.

Every organizational system has its own natural "immune system" whose task it is to resist unfamiliar, and so unrecognizable, signals. That is not bad per se. If the organization didn't have such an immune system, every alien "germ" would take root, and the organization wouldn't have enough stability to get anything done or enough continuity to give people the identity they need. But immune systems carry a price tag: even good germs get filtered out or killed off. The pre-transition immune system choked off creativity in its own manner, and no matter how loose and free the post-transition way of doing things is, its immune system will also make creativity difficult in some different way. It is during *the gap between the old and the new* that the organization's immune system is weak enough to let a seedbed for novelty form.

Innovation will take place automatically in the neutral zone if you provide people with the temporary structures discussed earlier and if you encourage them to find new ways to do things. Here are some ways in which you can actively encourage creativity.[3]

1. Establish by word and example that this is a time to step back and take stock, a time to question the "usual," and a time to come up with new and creative solutions to the organization's difficulties. Explain how business as usual chokes off creativity and explain why the present is the best possible time to generate and test new ideas. Model this new manner yourself by taking time to step back and question how your own job is done. Review those policies and procedures over which you have control. Your own example is your best leverage to change the behavior of others.

2. Provide opportunities for others to step back and take stock, both organizationally and individually: schedule retreats, policy reviews, surveys, and suggestion campaigns; offer people the chance to review their careers and refocus their efforts in areas of growing interest to them. If these activities generate new ideas for the organization, be sure to keep people informed

about what is being done with those ideas. Nothing undermines an effort like this faster than the appearance of good ideas being forgotten or not taken seriously.

3. Provide training in the techniques of discovery and innovation. This is the time for creative thinking courses and workshops on innovation. Too often such efforts fail to bear fruit, not because they are poorly done but because they are ill timed. They take place when the immune system is too strong. Now is the time to try them again. Some people simply don't know how to get out of their rut. Help them.

4. Encourage experimentation. People always have ideas that they have been wishing they had the chance to try, and they naturally generate solutions to problems they've been living with. What they seldom do, without encouragement and support, is try their ideas. Too often experimentation seems to people a risky undertaking that requires someone else's blessing. Give it yours. You'll be surprised how many improvements are just waiting for the chance to happen.

5. Embrace losses, setbacks, or disadvantages as entry points into new solutions. Steve Jobs and Steve Wozniak built their first Apple PC because they lacked the money to buy the computer-building kits that were "the right way" to build a computer in those days. Yamaha turned the sagging market for grand pianos into a challenge to come up with an electronic instrument that would mimic the sound and touch of the big piano perfectly. Brother took the deteriorating sewing machine market as a challenge to move into typewriters and other electronic instruments. Louisiana Pacific Corporation, which lacks the big timber stands of its major competitors, turned that lack to its advantage by shifting to the manufacture of boards and sheets made of gypsum and recycled paper.

6. Look for opportunities to brainstorm new answers to old problems. You have lived with them for so long that you may have unwittingly given up any hope of solving them. Break through this block, not by finding the single right answer but by finding 10 or 20 new answers—the crazier the better.

7. Finally, restrain the natural impulse in times of ambiguity and disorganization to push prematurely for certainty and closure. It is tempting to rally around, to have "everyone pulling together," in the neutral zone, but be

To exist is to change, to change is to mature, to mature is to go on creating oneself endlessly.

Henri Bergson,
French philosopher

When choosing between two evils, I always like to try the one I've never tried before.

Mae West,
American actress

The way to get good ideas is to get lots of ideas and throw the bad ones away.

Linus Pauling,
American chemist

careful that you don't unwittingly squeeze out dissent or other ways of thinking. You may even need to appoint a devil's advocate or an official critic of apparent consensus to see that people don't choke off new ideas in their desire to keep the team in one piece.

Whatever the details of the situation you face, the question to ask yourself is: *How can I make this interim between the old and the new not only a bearable time but a time during which the organization and everyone's place in it are enhanced? How can we come out of this waiting time better than we were before the transition started?* Here are some examples of doing that.

When you shift from one technological system to another, use the interim to redesign the work flow so that you aren't simply improving the technological means to an unimproved end.

When another company acquires yours, clarify your team's purpose and improve its functioning to maximize the chances that when the dust clears, it will be viewed as essential to the success of the acquiring company.

When you restructure your department, involve everyone in a no-holds-barred session of creative problem-solving in which roles are redefined and procedures are redesigned.

The generic advice is to turn every setback into an opportunity to improve things. The motto might be: "When orders fall, set people to work painting the factory." And don't bog down in getting everyone's blessing for your interim project. Such things are validated by their good results, and the good results are so much better than those of inaction that blessings almost always follow.

The key to succeeding in these efforts is to look at the neutral zone as a chance to do something new and interesting—and to pursue that goal with energy and courage.

To equip your people to take advantage of the opportunity for innovation that exists in the neutral zone, you need to foster a spirit of entrepreneurship among them. That spirit is totally alien to the "do what you're told" mood that characterizes many organizations, but an entrepreneurial outlook is the surest antidote to becoming frightened by change. It is entrepreneurial opportunism that spells the difference between success and failure in using the neutral zone creatively, and this opportunism depends on a willingness to

---

Where all think alike, no one thinks very much.

WALTER LIPPMANN, AMERICAN JOURNALIST

It is easier to get forgiveness than it is to secure permission.

JESUIT SAYING

Entrepreneurs see change as the norm and as healthy. Usually they do not bring about the change themselves. But—and this defines entrepreneur and entrepreneurship—the entrepreneur always searches for change, responds to it, and exploits it as opportunity.

PETER DRUCKER, AMERICAN MANAGEMENT EXPERT

take risks. That willingness, in turn, is not likely to develop without an organizational tolerance for intelligently conceived ventures that fail. In an organization that punishes failure, regardless of the value of the effort that failed, you aren't going to get this kind of effort. Be particularly careful that valuable concepts like "excellence" or "zero defects" don't get used as excuses to punish intelligent failures.

There is hardly a work project or procedure going on today in an American organization that couldn't be improved. In some sectors of the economy, the working principle is all old-fashioned bucket brigades and no hoses. Yet most efforts at getting "lean and mean" amount to little more than sending half the bucket brigade home and telling the rest of the bucket-handlers to work harder. A better answer is to use the time in the neutral zone creatively as an opportunity to redesign how you do what you do. If you do that, you will emerge from the wilderness both stronger and better adapted to your new environment. Neutral zone creativity is the key to turning transition from a time of breakdown into a time of breakthrough.

A Final Note on the Neutral Zone

Behind all this advice is an idea that can be validated with dozens of examples from both organizations and individual lives. During this apparently uneventful journey through the wilderness, a significant shift takes place within people—or if it doesn't, the change isn't likely to produce the results it is intended to. That shift comes from an inner repatterning and sorting process in which old and no longer appropriate habits are discarded and newly appropriate patterns of thought and action are developed.

In his book *Muddling Through,* Roger Golde tells a story that might stand as a fable about how this repatterning and sorting can take place in the neutral zone.[4] A French army unit was isolated in the Sahara Desert during World War II. Resupplying them was terribly difficult, and they were running out of everything. Their clothes were in particularly awful shape. Somehow a Red Cross clothing shipment reached them, but most of the clothes arrived with size labels that were illegible or missing, and everyone wondered how they could be matched to the people they would most nearly fit.

The commander, obviously an expert on neutral zone strategies, simply lined the troops up and issued each man one shirt, one pair of pants, and two

When old words die out on the tongue, new melodies break forth from the heart; and where the old tracks are lost, new country is revealed with its wonders.

RABINDRANATH TAGORE,
INDIAN PHILOSOPHER

shoes—with no attempt to fit for size or even to match pairs. Then he shouted, "Debrouillez-vous!" which means roughly, "Sort them out." There was a terrific scurrying and thrashing about while the men switched and swapped until they had clothes that more or less fit them. The result was a very adequate solution to an impossible problem—except for one unlucky soldier who ended up with two left shoes.

This story is a reminder that people can work out much of the necessary business of the neutral zone if you protect them, encourage them, and give them the structures and opportunities they need to do it.

Let's call that the neutral zone password: Debrouillez-vous!

Managing the Neutral Zone: A Checklist

Yes   No

___ ___ Have I done my best to normalize the neutral zone by explaining it as an uncomfortable time that (with careful attention) can be turned to everyone's advantage?

___ ___ Have I redefined the neutral zone by choosing a new and more affirmative metaphor with which to describe it?

___ ___ Have I reinforced that metaphor with training programs, policy changes, and financial rewards for people to keep doing their jobs during the neutral zone?

___ ___ Am I protecting people adequately from inessential further changes?

___ ___ If I can't protect them, am I clustering those changes meaningfully?

___ ___ Have I created the temporary policies and procedures that we need to get us through the neutral zone?

___ ___ Have I created the temporary roles, reporting relationships, and organizational groupings that we need to get us through the neutral zone?

___ ___ Have I set short-range goals and checkpoints?

___ ___ Have I set realistic output objectives?

____ ____ Have I found the special training programs we need to deal successfully with the neutral zone?

____ ____ Have I found ways to keep people feeling that they still belong to the organization and are valued by our part of it? And have I taken care that perks and other forms of "privilege" are not undermining the solidarity of the group?

____ ____ Have I set up one or more Transition Monitoring Teams to keep realistic feedback flowing upward during the time in the neutral zone?

____ ____ Are my people willing to experiment and take risks in intelligently conceived ventures—or are we punishing all failures?

____ ____ Have I stepped back and taken stock of how things are being done in my part of the organization? (This is worth doing both for its own sake and as a visible model for others' similar efforts.)

____ ____ Have I provided others with opportunities to do the same thing? Have I provided them with the resources—facilitators, survey instruments, and so on—that will help them do that?

____ ____ Have I seen to it that people build their skills in creative thinking and innovation?

____ ____ Have I encouraged experimentation and seen to it that people are not punished for failing in intelligent efforts that do not pan out?

____ ____ Have I worked to transform the losses of our organization into opportunities to try doing things a new way?

____ ____ Have I set an example by brainstorming many answers to old problems—the ones that people say we just have to live with? Am I encouraging others to do the same?

____ ____ Am I regularly checking to see that I am not pushing for certainty and closure when it would be more conducive to creativity to live a little longer with uncertainty and questions?

____ ____ Am I using my time in the neutral zone as an opportunity to replace bucket brigades with integrated systems throughout the organization?

Final Questions
What actions can you take to help people deal more successfully with the neutral zone in which your organization currently finds itself? What can you do today to get started on this aspect of transition management? (Write yourself a memo in the space below.)

---

1. The term comes from Arnold van Gennep's seminal study *Rites of Passage,* translated by Monika B. Vizedom and Gabrielle L. Chaffee (Chicago: University of Chicago Press, 1960). He applies it to the second (or middle) phase of tribal passage rites—those rites that help people to "cross over" one of life's natural dividing points. The crossover points that come at the end of childhood, when coming-of-age rituals are held, are the best known to modern, Western people. The same three-phase process of transformation is the basis for tribal rituals that take place at many other life-transition points. The parallel between tribal rituals and the three-phase transition process discussed here is more than simply an analogy, for one of the most useful ways of understanding what people experience when their organization changes (and they themselves are plunged into transition) is to say that they experience an *unritualized time of passage*—a time that was once ritualized but in our day has lost its ritual nature.

2. Cited in John Gardner and Francesca Gardner Reese, eds., *Quotations of Wit and Wisdom* (New York: W. W. Norton, 1975).

3. If you want to know more about creativity—a vast subject in itself—here are some of the books I have found useful:

> James L. Adams, *Conceptual Blockbusting* (Reading, MA: Addison-Wesley, 1986).
> William J. J. Gordon, *Synectics* (New York: Collier Books, 1961).
> William C. Miller, *The Creative Edge* (Reading, MA: Addison-Wesley, 1987).
> Roger von Oech, *A Whack on the Side of the Head* (New York: Warner Books, 1990).

4. Roger A. Golde, *Muddling Through: The Art of Properly Unbusiness Like Management* (New York: AMACOM Books, 1979).

Chapter Five

Launching a New Beginning

The only joy in the world is to begin.
—Cesare Pavese, Italian writer

The world fears a new experience more than it fears anything. Because a new experience displaces so many old experiences. . . . The world doesn't fear a new idea. It can pigeon-hole any idea. But it can't pigeon-hole a real new experience.
—D. H. Lawrence, British novelist

Beginnings are psychological phenomena. They are marked by a release of new energy in a new direction—they are the expression of a new identity. They are much more than the practical and situational "new circumstances" that we might call *starts*. On a situational level, things can be changed quickly:

The old computers are carted away, the new ones are installed, and everyone starts to get along without the old machines—though it takes quite a while before people are actually comfortable with the new ones.

The budget is cut and people start immediately working under new financial constraints, but they struggle for a good while to make them work—and keep complaining and talking about the Good Old Days when they had enough money to get things done right.

The day they put the new organization chart up on the wall, people know what their new roles are, who their new boss is, and who is on their team. In terms of the situational change, a new start is made on that very first day, but for weeks the old teams have a sort of shadow existence: people get together with old coworkers over coffee and go to their old bosses when they need advice about something.

In each of these cases, people haven't yet made a new *beginning*. They have just started something. Even though there is a new situation in place and they have started to grapple with it, people are still in the neutral zone feeling lost, confused, and uncertain. The *beginning* will take place only after they have come through the wilderness and are ready to make the emotional commitment to do things the new way and see themselves as new people. Starts involve new situations. Beginnings involve new understandings, new values, new attitudes, and—most of all—new identities.

Beginnings are always messy.

JOHN GALSWORTHY, BRITISH NOVELIST

A start can and should be carefully designed, like an object. A beginning can and should be nurtured, like a plant. Starts take place on a schedule as a result of decisions. They are signaled by announcements: "On March 25, the 24 district branches will be consolidated into 6 regional offices." Beginnings, on the other hand, are the final phase of this organic process that we call "transition," and their timing is not set by the dates written on an implementation schedule. Beginnings follow the timing of the mind and heart.

The change management plan will spell out the details of the start, but if it considers beginnings at all, it probably assumes that they happen automatically when people "get started doing the new things." Bosses always seem to assume the same thing, as they demonstrate when they say impatiently, "You guys have had *two weeks* to get the new computer system [or the new self-managed teams, etc.] up and going! Your people don't seem to be *with it*. What's the problem?" They're confusing starts with beginnings.

Ambivalence Toward Beginnings

Beginnings are strange things. People want them to happen but fear them at the same time. After long and seemingly pointless wanderings through the neutral zone, most people are greatly relieved to arrive at whatever Promised Land they've been moving toward. Yet beginnings are also scary, for they require a new commitment. They require, in some sense, that people become the new kind of person that the new situation demands. There are a number of reasons people resist new beginnings, even though they may be attracted by the idea of making them.

1. Beginnings reactivate some of the old anxieties that were originally triggered by the ending. Beginnings, after all, establish once and for all that

an ending was real. I may, for example, be "absolutely sure" that my old relationship is finished—until I start having second thoughts after beginning a new one. There is always something provisional about a decision to stop doing something until you have actually replaced it with something else. A new beginning "ratifies" the ending. (That finality is paradoxically also the source of excitement, for it signals that you've made a clean break and have the chance to begin again from scratch.)

2. The new way of doing things represents a gamble: there is always the possibility it won't work. The very idea of doing something the new way may be crazy, or it may be unrealistic to think that an individual or a group can carry it off. They (or worse yet, you) may even make a shameful mess of the effort.

3. The prospect of a risky new beginning will probably resonate with the past. On a personal level, it may trigger old memories of failures that destroyed your self-esteem. Organizationally, it may resonate with a history in which failures have been punished or with a specific incident in which a new beginning was aborted in some traumatic fashion.

4. Finally, for some people new beginnings destroy what was a pleasant experience in the neutral zone. Most people don't like the wilderness, but a few find the ambiguity "interesting" and the slower pace of work rather pleasant. Or else the confusion gives them a cover under which to conceal their own lack of interest in the tasks at hand, and the absence of a clear agenda gives them an excuse for their inactivity. For such people, the new beginning is an end to a pleasant holiday from accountability and pressure.

One of the greatest pains to human nature is the pain of a new idea.

WALTER BAGEHOT, BRITISH POLITICAL SCIENTIST

The Timing of New Beginnings

Like any organic process, beginnings cannot be made to happen by a word or act. They happen when the timing of the transition process allows them to happen, just as flowers and fruit appear on a schedule that is natural and not subject to anyone's will. That is why it is so important to understand the transition process and where people are in it.

There go my people. I must find out where they are going so that I can lead them.

ALEXANDRE LEDRU-ROLLIN, FRENCH POLITICIAN

Only when you get into people's shoes and feel what they are feeling can you help them to manage their transition. More beginnings abort because they were not preceded by well-managed endings and neutral zones than for any other reason.

But if beginnings cannot be forced according to your personal wishes, they can be encouraged, supported, and reinforced. You can't turn a key or flip a switch, but you can cultivate the ground and provide the nourishment. What you can do falls under four headings:

1. You can explain the basic *purpose* behind the outcome you seek. People have to understand the logic of it before they will turn their minds to work on it.

2. You can paint a *picture* of how the outcome will look and feel. People need to experience it imaginatively before they can give their hearts to it.

3. You can lay out a step-by-step *plan* for phasing in the outcome. People need a clear idea of how they can get where they need to go.

4. You can give each person a *part* to play in both the plan and the outcome. People need a tangible way to contribute and participate.

Do unto others as they would be done unto.

"THE GOLDEN RULE," MODIFIED

To make a new beginning, in other words, people need the Four P's: the purpose, a picture, the plan, and a part to play. For any particular individual, one or sometimes two of these P's will predominate. Your own path into the future probably emphasizes one of these Four P's—and minimizes or even omits others. As a result, you will tend to stress your own preference(s) when you communicate with others. You may naturally assume that others approach beginnings the way you do, but that isn't necessarily so. People are really different—they aren't just "defective" versions of yourself. So it is important to remember to cover all four of these bases—purpose, picture, plan, and part—when you talk about the new beginning you're trying to help people make.

If you cry, "Forward," you must make clear the direction in which to go. Don't you see that if you fail to do that and simply call out the word to a monk and a revolutionary, they will go in precisely the opposite directions.

ANTON CHEKHOV, RUSSIAN WRITER

Clarify and Communicate the Purpose

What is the idea behind what you're doing? The idea behind Moses's journey through the wilderness was that God had promised his people, who had been persecuted in their adopted home of Egypt, a land of their own; that promise was something everyone could understand. This promise was a solution to problems they had experienced and an answer to the question: "Why are we doing this?" It represented a clear purpose for their journey.

You need to explain the purpose behind the new beginning clearly. You may discover that people have trouble understanding the purpose because they do not have a realistic idea of where the organization really stands and what its problems are. In that case, you need to "sell the problems" before you try to sell a solution to those problems. If that wasn't done during the ending phase—when it should have been done—now is the time to provide answers to these questions:

What is the problem? What is the situation that requires this change to solve it?

Who says so, and on what evidence?

What would occur if no one acted to solve this problem?

And what would happen to us if that occurred?

There is almost always some purpose behind a change, though sometimes you need to adapt that purpose to the interests and understandings of your audience. An increase in shareholder value is not an idea that means much to rank-and-file workers unless it is presented in terms of its effect on their security, pay, or working conditions. The same is true for such important ideas as quality improvement, customer satisfaction, and increased profitability.

One of the terrible obstacles to many beginnings is that there is no discernible purpose behind the proposed changes. There are different reasons for an apparent lack of purpose, and each of them calls for a different action from you.

The purpose is not discernible because it has not yet been clearly explained in terms that mean something to you. That may be because the purpose was not effectively communicated or because people did not understand the explanation. In either case, provide (or ask for) more explanation, making it clear that you are not questioning the intent but that you need more help in communicating it to your people. This problem may also arise because the question of purpose has not been thought through clearly enough to be effectively communicated. You should still ask for more

> *Great minds have purposes, others have wishes.*
>
> WASHINGTON IRVING, AMERICAN WRITER

explanation, though the answer may be trickier because the leaders may have to face the fact that they aren't yet clear themselves.

The purpose is not discernible because it has not been communicated at all. There are three main reasons this happens:

1. There may be no purpose, at least none that will stand up to open scrutiny. The change may have been someone's whim. It may have been an attempt to show that the leadership is not passive. It may have been initiated because the organization next door did it. It may have been the result of drawing straws in the boardroom. If you decide there isn't a valid purpose behind the change, it is going to be very hard to bring people out of the neutral zone. Circle the wagons and figure out how best to use your time until the decisionmaking process gets back on track.

2. There *is* an idea, but the leadership isn't talking because they don't think that people need to understand . . . or that they don't need to understand *now.* Sooner or later most leaders who take this approach lose their followers. If you're lucky, it will be sooner rather than later, because then something will have to happen. But in the meantime, if feedback to your superiors has no effect, follow the advice given in the foregoing paragraph.

3. There is a purpose—at least you strongly suspect there is—but the "official reason" is a smoke screen to cover what cannot publicly be said. The technical term for this is "lying," and its long-term effects on people are very bad. They lose trust in their leaders, they withdraw their loyalty, they grow resentful, the best of them leave, and the weaker ones sit around imagining ways to pay the organization back for its dishonesty. At best, such an effort simply fails. What can you do in such cases? Often, not much. But sometimes you can get your company's executives to see that the truth is not as terrifying as they imagine. Sometimes you can help them figure out how to tell the truth—or at least stop lying—without wrecking everything. Failing that, you can try, without slitting your own throat, to disengage yourself from the lying.

Sometimes you may find yourself falling back on the age-old explanation, "The boss wants us to do it," or, "If we don't do it, we're all fired." Few organizations run for long on such purposes, but those sentiments can be strong motivators for short bursts of activity.

Perhaps the situation is not so dark as in these scenarios. Let's assume, for example, that you're involved in the decisionmaking and so have some influence in setting and defining the purpose behind the action. Bear these things in mind:

The purpose must be real, not make-believe. When budget cuts—necessitating a draconian downsizing—are described as a way to "improve operations" (as they were in an organization where my firm recently worked), you're simply sowing mistrust and cynicism at a time when you're going to need all the commitment and energy you can muster.

The purpose needs to grow out of the actual situation faced by the organization and the organization's nature and resources. Today many different purposive ideas are fashionable:

- "We're going for *excellence.*"

- "We're going to be a *cutting-edge* company."

- "We're going to be *number one* in the industry."

- "We're going to be the *low-cost producer* (or the *value-added leader* or the *customer-service champ*)."

These are clichés. The words mean something, but the speakers who use them usually do not. If they did, they would say what they mean and not what everyone else is saying these days. When SAS Airlines said that customer service was the key, when Ford said that quality was the key—when any organization has said what its own leadership really believed—everyone listened. But when organizations simply repeat some widely touted purposive idea of the day, all the employees hear is, "Me too."

The kind of purpose that you will need in order to launch a new beginning must come from within the organization—from its will, abilities, resources, and character. To be more specific, it must arise from the way in which these inherent qualities interact with the situation in which the organization finds itself. It is that interaction that spells opportunity in a changing world. If your purpose is simply copied from another organization, or if it belies the real situation in which the organization finds itself, it won't do its job.

Just because everything is different doesn't mean that anything has changed.

Irene Peter,
American writer

Successful new beginnings are based on a clear and appropriate purpose. Without one, there may be lots of starts but no real beginnings. In fact, there may be one start after another in a sequence of changes that tire everyone out without solving the underlying problems. Without a beginning, the transition is incomplete. And without transition, the change changes nothing.

After a Purpose, a Picture

Purposes are critical to beginnings, but they are rather abstract. They are *ideas,* and most people are not ready to throw themselves into a difficult and risky undertaking simply on the basis of an idea.[1] They need something they can see, at least in their imaginations. They need a *picture* of how the outcome will look, and they need to be able to imagine how it will feel to be a participant in it.

This picture in people's heads is the reality they live in, and one of the losses that takes place during the ending phase of a transition is that the old picture—the mental image of how and why things are the way they are—falls apart. Much of the pain of the neutral zone comes from the fact that it is a time without a viable organizational picture. (Part of the task of neutral zone management is to create a "temporary wilderness" picture in people's minds, a picture that explains and validates what they are experiencing.) It is the new organizational picture that refocuses people's energies and brings them out of the neutral zone with a new sense of their collective identity and a new meaning for their efforts.

So your second task is to create this picture.[2] There is nothing mystical or artistic about this process. Moses, who was so self-doubting about his ability to inspire others that he tried to turn down Jehovah's call to lead the Jewish people, did it very effectively. He translated the *idea* of a Promised Land into the *picture* of a Land of Milk and Honey. He did not stop with creating an understanding of the destination; he portrayed the destination in a way that engaged the Israelites' imaginations.

What will the outcome of the change you're trying to manage look like and sound like? How will people get their work done and interact with each other? What will the spatial layout of the place be like? How will a day at this place be organized? When people first encounter the new way of doing things, what impression will it make on them? What feeling will they get just from being there? In other words, what will people *experience* that is different?

A rock pile ceases to be a rock pile the moment a single man contemplates it, bearing within him the image of a cathedral.

ANTOINE DE SAINT-EXUPÉRY, FRENCH NOVELIST

Use visual aids to convey the picture of the new way things will be. A floor plan of the new office layout, a picture of the new automated packaging line, a video of a self-managed team planning the coming month's priorities, a map showing the expanded area served by the branches of the merged banks—these aids help people to imagine what the new way will be like. Another way to paint a picture is to arrange for people to visit another organization where things are already done in the new way. As they see and talk with people like themselves working successfully under the new conditions, they can begin to visualize and feel at home with the new way.

Two Things to Watch Out For

A couple of warnings about helping your people visualize the new way. First, don't expect the picture to have its effect prematurely—that is, before your people have made an ending and let go of the past. There is no harm (and there is actual gain) in showing the picture to people as soon as the change is announced. Doing so will plant the picture of the future in their imaginations, where it will reassure them. But it does not make the transition happen. It was not the image of the Land of Milk and Honey that got the people out of Egypt or through the wilderness to the Promised Land—it was Moses's skill as a transition leader.

Misplaced faith in the picture's power to make a transition happen is encouraged by a misunderstanding that is common among people who design change projects. Such people typically go through *their* transitions before they launch the changes, while they're still struggling with the problems and searching for solutions. By the time they are ready to announce the change, they have long since put their endings and their neutral zone behind them, and now they're ready for a new beginning. But they forget that middle management is probably just entering the neutral zone and that most workers have not even made their endings yet.

This situation might be called "the marathon effect"—it is similar to what happens in road races with thousands of runners. The front runners take off like rabbits, then the second rank (who are a little slower anyway) start running, and then the middle ranks (who are nowhere near as fast) get under way. By the time the leaders are well out on the course, the Sunday runners in the rear, who were too far back even to hear the starting gun (and who only hope to be able to finish the race) are beginning to stir. A rumor comes back through the crowd: the race has started. The Sunday runners move their feet a

Hope is generally a wrong guide, though it is very good company by the way.

Charles Montagu,
Earl of Halifax,
British statesman

little to loosen up, but they can't really run yet. They shuffle a little, then begin taking small steps.

About the time the Sunday runners have speeded up to a slow jog, some of the front runners are nearing the finish line and thinking, *Well, this is about over. Good race. What'll I do next week?* So it is with the company executives. They went through *their* transitions long ago when they started grappling with the problems. They forget that their followers are still struggling.

The second warning is not to overwhelm people with a picture that is so hard for them to identify with that they become intimidated rather than excited by it. One of my firm's clients presented a videotape of a new automated production line like the one that was going to be installed in the plant we were working with. The tape was made by a fancy outfit in Hollywood and featured stirring music from the broadcasts of the recently completed Los Angeles Olympic Games. The workers watched dramatic angle shots of their product speeding through space-age machinery, and they saw people studying computer printouts that they could not even imagine being able to understand. The result was that most of the audience left thinking they couldn't do the work.

The same manufacturing plant got a much better result from a visual aid that cost perhaps a twentieth as much as the video. It was a wonderfully detailed scale model of the new automated production line with little people and little cases of products that could be moved around. It was set up in the factory lunchroom, where workers could see it every day and even play with it. Before long the toy workers were tagged with the names of actual employees, and people were beginning to picture themselves at work in the new setting.

Now Create a Plan

Some people really respond to the picture. Once they get it in their heads, they find a way to reach the destination that has captured their imagination. Many executives and planners fall into this group, and because they don't feel as much of a personal need for a plan that spells out the details of the route from *here* to *there,* they underestimate how much others need such a plan. For many operationally minded people, the picture is interesting, but the real question is, "What do we do on Monday?"

The plan I am talking about is not the large-scale outline of stages and dates—which explains when, for example, the new automated machinery will be ordered, when it will arrive, when it will be installed, and when the first shipment of goods manufactured the new way will be shipped. That is the plan for the *changes,* not the *transitions.* The plan I am talking about outlines the steps and schedule in which people will receive the information, training, and support they need to make the transition. It lays out the nature and timing of key events that mark the phases of the transition: a ceremony marking the closure of an old facility or the disbanding of a group, the formation of a transition monitoring team, the scheduling of a visit to another site, an all-hands question-and-answer session with the site manager, the start of a training program, the date of a planning retreat or brainstorming session, and the like.

The transition management plan differs from the change management plan in several ways. First, it is much more detailed, addressing the change on the personal rather than the collective level. It is much more person-oriented because it tells José, Sally, and Ray how and when their worlds are going to change. Second, it is oriented to the process and not just the outcome. It lays out the details of what's going to be done to help those individuals deal with the effects of the changes. It tells them when they can expect to receive information and training, and how and when they can have input into the planning process.

A third difference is less evident in the final product but important in its creation. A change management plan starts with the outcome and then works backward, step by step, to create the necessary preconditions for that outcome. A transition management plan, on the other hand, starts with where people are and works forward, step by step, through the process of leaving the past behind, getting through the wilderness and profiting from it, and emerging with new attitudes, behaviors, and identity. A transition management plan can be put together by selecting, designing, and scheduling events, actions, and projects from the possibilities that are listed in chapters 3, 4, and 5.

Finally, a Part to Play

Plans are immensely reassuring to most people, not just because they contain information but because they exist. As is noted in the Book of Exodus, in the wilderness of the neutral zone people "murmured." One of the things they must have murmured was, "Do you think Moses has any *plan,* or do you think he's making this up as he goes along?" The existence of the plan sends a message: somebody is looking after us, taking our needs seriously, and watching out so we don't get lost along the way.

But even the best-laid plans leave a troubling doubt in the minds of some people. They don't see *their* names on the wall chart. No one has told them how *they* fit into the new scheme of things. No one has given *them* any role to play in the journey itself. The purpose, the picture, and the plan all omit something: a part for them to play. Until that is provided, many people will feel left out and will find it difficult to make a new beginning.

You'll usually need to give people two parts to play. First, they need to see the role and their relationship to others in the new scheme of things. If their name appears on the new organization chart, they may not like where you have put them, but it beats not seeing their name on the chart at all. Until people know the parts they are to play, they can't begin the slow process of adjusting their hopes and fears to the new reality. Until they know their parts, fantasies dictate their actions and can lead them far from the new realities they will be facing.

But that is only the part people will play in the *outcome*. You also need to give people a role in dealing effectively with the transition process itself. The easiest way to do this is to be sure that everyone has some role on one of the planning task forces, climate survey groups, problem-solving circles, or transition monitoring teams. If this is not possible, set up formal input systems for such groupings so that each person has at least an indirect part to play in the transition management process. This is particularly important for people who have lost some significant part that they played in the old order (see chapter 3, "Compensate for the Losses").

Giving people a significant part to play in the transition management process facilitates the new beginning in five ways:

1. It gives people new insight into the real problems being faced by the organization as it comes out of the neutral zone and redefines itself. When people understand problems, they are in the market for solutions.

2. By sharing these problems, you align yourself and your subordinates on one side and the problems on the other. The polarity is not between you and them; you are allies, not adversaries. If relationships have been frayed by change, this is a chance to rebuild them.

3. Giving people a part brings their firsthand knowledge to bear on solving problems. Joint decisions are not necessarily better than unilateral ones, but including people makes their knowledge available to the decision-maker, whoever that may be.

4. The knowledge thus provided is more than the facts about the problem—it also includes the facts about the self-interest of the various parties affected by the situation. Outcomes work best if they serve (or at least don't violate) the self-interest of the participants. Without that knowledge, the results are likely to be solutions that, however technically or economically satisfactory, run afoul of human issues.

5. Finally, everyone who plays a part is, tacitly at least, implicated in the outcome. That is, after all, how democracy works: you vote, and your vote is an implicit promise to abide by the results. Although actual votes are rare in the organizational world, this essential strength of democracy is still attainable and advantageous. As in the political arena, it is more important that people accept the solution, whatever it is, than that it is the ideal solution. In most cases, excellence is about seven parts commitment and three parts strategy.

Reinforcing the New Beginning

All of these tactics help people to leave the disturbing and creative chaos of the neutral zone and refocus their energies in new directions. They help people to shape new identities to replace the ones they gave up when they let go of how things used to be. But that refocusing needs to be reinforced if it is to keep its new shape and not revert to chaos when the initial focus is impacted by the continuing stream of changes that will surely come along.[3]

Rule 1: Be Consistent

The first form of reinforcement is consistency of message. Every policy, procedure, and list of priorities sends a message, but if you aren't careful, your messages will be conflicting ones.

> If you say that office automation requires a "paperless workflow" and then require typed reports on the progress toward that end, you're sending conflicting messages.

If you tell people that a budget crunch requires them to buy pencils and paper clips with their own money, while the organization's executives are still flying first class, you're sending conflicting messages.

If you tell people they need to do five new things but don't remove anything from their list of tasks, you're sending conflicting messages. (Telling them to do more with less is simply telling them to cut corners in what may be very dangerous ways. Telling them to work smarter is telling them to do more with less.)

Conflicting messages are confusing in their own right and also provide people with excuses to argue that the new beginning isn't for real.

The second form of reinforcement is a particular kind of consistency: the consistency of your own actions. Regardless of the confusions surrounding a new beginning—and you're sure to have your own share—you have one reliable point of leverage in moving people out of the neutral zone: the example of your own behavior.

Example is not the main thing in influencing others, it's the only thing.

ALBERT SCHWEITZER, FRENCH PHILOSOPHER-PHYSICIAN

An example used in chapter 2 illustrates the problem. In that case a promising new beginning was imperiled by a leader who didn't realize how much louder actions speak than words. Anxious to reorganize his people into service teams that integrated formerly separate layers of service techs, that leader ceaselessly preached the benefits of teamwork and collective decisionmaking. But the direct reports on his own staff, each of whom was being told to transform his group into a team, was run as a set of one-on-one relationships between the executive and the person who reported to him.

The third form of reinforcement is another kind of consistency. It is common (and always disastrous) to tell people to act and react in new ways—and then to reward them acting and reacting in the old ways. You won't manage to hold a new beginning for long:

It is difficult to get a man to understand something when his salary depends upon his not understanding it.

UPTON SINCLAIR, AMERICAN WRITER

- If you preach teamwork and then reward individual contributions

- If you preach customer service and then reward "following the rules"

- If you preach risk-taking and then reward "no mistakes"

- If you preach feedback and then reward "no criticism"

- If you preach entrepreneurship and then reward "doing your job"

- If you preach decentralized authority and then reward hands-on management

The rewards in question are not just financial ones, and that is good news, because the financial rewards may have been legally set in the last contract negotiation. But many of the most important rewards were not, including all the "strokes" that people receive: their boss's time and attention, perks and privileges, praise and awards, additional training, and interesting development opportunities. People have to feel that they are better off for having changed their attitudes and behavior. If they don't, you'd better look at your reward system.

Rule 2: Ensure Quick Successes

The neutral zone takes a heavy toll on most people's self-confidence because it is a period of lowered productivity and diminished feelings of competence. It may also, if it resonates with past difficulties in a person's life, activate serious problems of low self-esteem. For that reason people are likely to need some fairly quick successes if they are to return to their former effectiveness.

These successes can come from small tasks, which can be accomplished even in spite of the damaged self-confidence of transition survivors. They can come from sure wins—situations with little risk of failure. They can even come from ongoing efforts where success was pretty well in the bag before people took them over.

A benefit of quick successes is that when changes are deep and far-reaching, new beginnings take a long time to be fully realized. Believers may begin to doubt, and doubters turn into critics. Critics then have a field day. Quick successes reassure the believers, convince the doubters, and confound the critics.

Rule 3: Symbolize the New Identity

People are not merely logical beings; they are full of feeling too. They are not just literal-minded; they also react symbolically to events. That is why apparently small things can take on enormous importance as individuals and their organization struggle to make new beginnings work. Two mergers that we worked on provide examples of this.

In the first case, a serious conflict arose over whether identification badges at the newly integrated company would be blue (like the old ones at the larger company) or white (like those at the smaller but more successful company). It was decided to make them gold to mirror the new identity. The result: no more conflict and a successful merger. In the second case, one organization was combining with another, and the same conflict erupted over parking stickers. This time it wasn't a true merger: the upper management of the first company was going to run the combined show, and only the supervisors and lower-level employees of the second company were coming aboard. The decision was to start with the old parking sticker of the acquiring organization but to use a different typeface on it.

The point is not that such symbolism contributes to success, but simply that it conveys a message that reinforces the new identity being established in the new organizational beginning. During highly charged times of transition, everything takes on a symbolic hue—everything *means something*. That can trip you up because you don't intend to mean something with everything you do. At the same time, you can use it to your advantage by viewing everything symbolically and looking for opportunities to symbolize the new beginning you are trying to make.

Rule 4: Celebrate the Success

Finally, take time to celebrate arriving in the Promised Land. Just as you marked the endings at the start of transition, you need to mark the beginning at the finish of transition. The timing may seem a little arbitrary because there are always loose ends to be tied up. But when you feel that the majority of your people are emerging from the wilderness and that a new purpose, a new system, and a new sense of identity have been established, you'll do well to take time to celebrate that the transition is over. It may be something as small as a get-together on Friday afternoon or something as big as a victory trip with spouses to Acapulco. In either case, it should be fun and a break from the routine.

It's not a bad idea to let people take away something from this celebration too, a memento of the transition process that is now behind them. The idea is not unlike giving people a piece of the past, as mentioned in chapter 3. In this case it may be a T-shirt with "I Survived the Merger" across the front or a certificate of thanks for their participation in the Transition Monitoring Team. Serious or humorous, the memento further acknowledges and winds up a difficult time in the organization's history and the person's career.

Conclusion

Behind all of these tactics is the basic idea with which we began, an idea that is more important than any of the tactics themselves: things *start* when the plan says they will, but the *new beginning* takes place much more slowly. If transition is mishandled or if it is overlooked completely, beginnings often fail to take place. In such cases, we say that "the change didn't work," or that it "fell short of our expectations." What we ought to say is that we got the people out of Egypt but they're still wandering somewhere in the wilderness.

Managing the New Beginning: A Checklist

Yes   No

___ ___ Am I distinguishing in my own mind, and in my expectations of others, between the start, which can happen on a planned schedule, and the beginning, which will not?

___ ___ Do I accept the fact that people are going to be ambivalent toward the beginning I am trying to bring about?

___ ___ Have I taken care of the ending(s) and the neutral zone, or am I trying to make a new beginning happen before it possibly can?

___ ___ Have I clarified and communicated the *purpose* of (the idea behind) the change?

___ ___ Have I drawn an effective *picture* of the change's outcome and found ways to communicate it effectively?

___ ___ Have I created a *plan* for bringing people through the three phases of transition—and distinguished it in my own mind from the change management plan?

___ ___ Have I helped people to discover as soon as possible the *part* that they will play in the outcome of these changes, and how that outcome will affect the part they currently play within the organization?

___ ___ Have I ensured that everyone has a part to play in the transition management process and that they understand their part?

____ ____ Have I checked to see that policies, procedures, and priorities are consistent with the new beginning I am trying to make so that inconsistencies aren't sending a mixed message?

____ ____ Am I watching my own actions carefully to be sure that I am effectively modeling the attitudes and behaviors I am asking others to develop?

____ ____ Have I found ways, financial and nonfinancial, to reward people for becoming the new people I am calling upon them to become?

____ ____ Have I built into my plans some occasions for quick success to help people rebuild their self-confidence and to build the image of the transition as successful?

____ ____ Have I found ways to celebrate the new beginning and the conclusion of the time of transition?

____ ____ Have I found ways to symbolize the new identity—organizational and personal—that is emerging from this period of transition?

____ ____ Have I given people a piece of the transition to keep as a reminder of the difficult and rewarding journey we all took together?

Final Questions

What actions could you take to help people deal more successfully with the new beginnings they must make if your change effort is to succeed? What could you do today to get started on this aspect of transition management? (Write yourself a memo in the space below.)[4]

1. Some are ready to, and if they happen to be the organization's leaders, they are unlikely to realize that other people do not respond to ideas as viscerally as they do. They may put out the idea and then wonder why people are holding back. They need to see that ideas alone only galvanize idea-minded people. Others need one or more of the other three Ps: pictures, plans, and a part to play.

2. As I use the term, "picture" has a lot in common with what today is called an organizational "vision." But I use "picture" because "vision" has become associated with "visionary" and is often used in an almost mystical way to refer to something that has the power—almost by itself—to revitalize an organization and to realign its people. I don't buy that. Too many visions are pure fantasy that simply alienate leaders from their more down-to-earth followers. Just as relatively few people can be swept up and moved to action by an idea alone, so it is with only a vision to go on.

In the typological categories created by Carl Jung, *thinking* types can be activated by an idea and *intuitive* types can be activated by a vision. But *sensate* types need a plan, and *feeling* types need everyone to have a part in the undertaking.

3. See chapter 6 for specific ways to deal with continuous change.

4. Note that you may not be far enough into the process of transition to find many of these tactics timely yet. Don't worry. Just utilize the ones that are appropriate to your situation, and use the rest as a checklist for future action. Build them into your transition-management plan.

Chapter Six

Transition, Development, and Renewal

People, products, markets, even societies, have life-cycles—birth, growth, maturity, old age, and death. At every life-cycle passage a typical pattern of behavior emerges. . . . As the organization passes from one phase of its life to the next, different roles are emphasized and the different role combinations that result produce different organizational behaviors. . . . The [life-cycle] model enables an organization to foresee the problems it will face as it grows over time. Furthermore, it . . . presents a framework for prescribing the treatments most likely to be effective depending on the life-cycle stage of the organization.

ICHAK ADIZES, "ORGANIZATIONAL PASSAGES"[1]

The idea that organizations and societies have life cycles has been around a long time.[2] When we say that General Motors is "older" than Intel, we mean more than that it was established longer ago. We talk about Europe as the *Old* World and America as the *New* World, and again, we mean more than chronology. A start-up biotech company exists in the part of the organizational lifetime that we think of as its "childhood"; we talk about an organization or a society going through an "adolescent" phase; and everyone has a pretty good idea what we mean when we talk about a "mature" business or one that is approaching "the end of its life."

The organizational life cycle also provides an important way to understand some of the larger significance of many specific transitions. An ending that launches a transition may be traumatic, not just because of the particular set of circumstances surrounding it, but because it winds up an important chapter of the organization's life. And the difficulty that an organization has launching a new beginning may come less from the new situation that has to

Life is a process of becoming, a combination of states we have to go through. Where people fail is that they wish to elect a state and remain in it. This is a kind of death.

ANAÏS NIN,
AMERICAN DIARIST

be managed than from the fact that the new beginning represents a whole new life stage for the organization and a new and unfamiliar identity.

To understand transition from this perspective, it is helpful to have a map of the organization's life cycle that is comparable to the human development theories that clarify the path an individual follows through human childhood, adolescence, and adulthood. Without such a map, a teenager's life would look like a crazy set of purely personal problems that just happened to occur at the end of childhood. Just as the term "adolescence" helps us to understand what is really going on in a young person's life, so the different segments of the organizational life cycle can help organizational development (OD) specialists, and the leaders with whom they consult, to understand not only why the organization is encountering certain kinds of problems when it does, but also what they need to do about them.

Ironically, what OD professionals call organizational "development" has very little to do with the organization's movement through this life cycle. Instead, it usually involves various kinds of organizational "improvements." Better communication, wider participation in decisionmaking, and a less authoritarian style of leadership are typical OD goals, and none of them is a *developmental* issue in the sense we are talking about.[3] This is not just a quibble about definition: the failure of the field of organizational development to deal with real "developmental" issues has left people confused about the larger significance of transition, which is that it is the transformative process by which an organization—or a part of it, anything from a project team to an international division—becomes more complex and better adapted to its environment.

I have a great belief in the fact that whenever there is chaos, it creates wonderful thinking. I consider chaos a gift.

Septima Poinsette Clark, American civil rights activist

The Seven Stages of Organizational Life

Shakespeare wrote about the "Seven Ages of Man." Here are seven comparable stages of organizational life.[4]

The point is not that these seven stages and their names are God-given realities that represent fixed times in an organization's life. You could come up with a list of six or twelve stages and give them very different names, and you might have just as useful a map. I have used this particular one for more than twenty years, and I find it very helpful in working with organizations in transition. Try it out in your own work, and see if it doesn't clarify things.

Age seldom arrives smoothly or quickly. It's more often in a succession of jerks.

Jean Rhys, British novelist

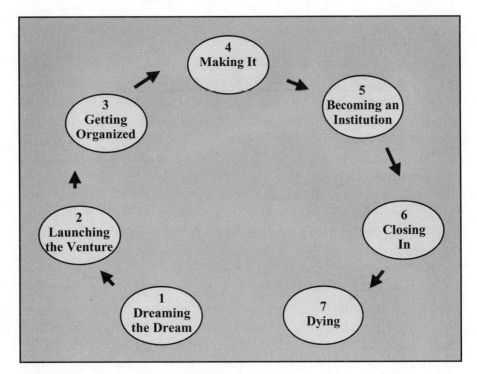

Figure 6.1   The organizational life cycle.

1. Dreaming the Dream

The first stage is the time of imagining and planning, when the organization is little more than an idea in the mind of the founders. This is the time when the main activities are articulating the Dream and trying to get people to join in bringing it into physical existence and to contribute money to the task of realizing it. A lot of time is spent sitting around people's offices and living rooms, brainstorming and arguing. There may or may not be a demonstrable "product" yet, for the organization itself is "in utero." The Dream lasts until it is given up—and many dreams never grow beyond this first phase—or until it is born as a Venture.

2. Launching the Venture

This time is the organization's infancy and childhood. Birth has taken place, the Venture is "out there," people may even be starting to buy the products. If they are, the Venture will be growing—perhaps very rapidly. Some ventures end up serving large numbers of customers even before they move on to their next phase. They may be raking in money. What makes them "ventures" is not that they are not yet successful, but that they are doing whatever they are doing by the seat of their pants at this stage. There are no formal systems yet—no hiring policies or pay scales, no fixed way of doing things. The organization may actually be little more than a bunch of people sharing a letterhead and a checking account.

The people who thrive in this phase of the organization's life cycle are good at improvising. Many of those people (they'll be called "old-timers" one day) subsequently look back on these days with affection—"Wasn't that *fun,* back when we all did everything and no one knew what the rules were?" People may have titles for the sake of the business cards, but the titles mean little, and they may still be living off their savings while they try to attract enough capital to take off.

Some Ventures do really take off (Apple Computer was a $1 billion a year company before it left the Venture phase), while others move forward much more slowly. In either case, you can go only so far by "making it up as you go" before the database is a mess, the computers don't network, and people are angry because there is no logic to who's paid how much. Before these problems sink you, you need to Get Organized.

3. Getting Organized

To some people this stage feels like a step backward, since many of the ways to bring order to a chaotic situation force you to slow down and do things in some standardized way. For people who've been toting around a pocketful of the business cards that people give them on sales calls, working out a reliable way to get the names into a contact management program and learning to use the program to follow up regularly on sales contacts may feel like the first step toward "bureaucracy." But the company has come to the point where the natural energy of the founders is no longer enough to ensure continued good results. The frantic efforts of a handful of people need to be replaced by a more predictable set of activities by a growing number of people.

This is the time when roles start to become more specialized and more formally defined. It is the time when financial controls are established, when employment policies are spelled out, when company publications become more than fund-raising efforts. New kinds of people are hired, people who have actually already done what you're asking them to do now. The hiring process changes as experience starts to become more important—though the old-timers may feel that such people are the carriers of something dangerous and alien to the wonderful, homegrown, "part-of-the-family" quality that characterizes a Venture. Getting Organized isn't easy, and a few companies and institutions run aground in the process. But most of them survive and come out of this phase with the new structures, practices, systems, agreements, and habits that they need to take their places in the world of "grown-up" organizations. When that happens, the organization enters the next phase of its life.

4. Making It

This is the point when the organization's "adulthood" begins. From this point on, the organization has what it needs to be a significant factor in its market. An organization that is successfully Making It can expand and grow more complex for a very long time without ever leaving this stage. But this is the point at which it begins to reap the rewards of its successful early development in the form of financial success, workforce growth, an expanding product line, and an increasing reputation for whatever it does. It may face serious (even daunting) competition, but it is now established in its market. It has a solid foothold and the basis for continuing expansion. There can be many subchapters to this time in the organization's life as growth leads to problems, which necessitate changes, which lead to further growth. But through it all, the organization's fundamental nature continues.

Or it continues until the kinds of successes that it achieves begin to seem less attractive for its leaders than does the intangible "institutional" quality that some of its older competitors or the famous organizations in other fields have. People start to feel that these other, more mature organizations have "something that we don't." They have more significance, more importance, more *class*. Often this feeling of lack gets attached to tangible things: "An organization of our importance needs a bigger headquarters building . . . a corporate jet . . . a logo with a more 'classic' look."[5] This dissatisfaction is not like the earlier signals that it was time to move to the next phase. That is, it does not signify that the old way has reached the limit of its usefulness or that it's no longer working. The dissatisfaction is more a matter of style than of substance, but it is no less compelling for that. It is a feeling that it is time for the organization to take its place as not just a successful organization in its field but as one of the Big Boys—as an Institution.

5. Becoming an Institution

This shift is subtle but profound: the emphasis moves from doing to being, from the results that the organization achieves to the external impression that it makes. The organizational imperative shifts from that of taking and staking out territory to occupying it. People talk more and more about how things ought to be done in "an organization like this" and about what is appropriate to an organization that occupies a place like this one. The shift may be so subtle as to pass almost unnoticed, but new hires start being chosen less for their talent and motivation and more for how they will fit in with "us." Reputation is something that the organization has—it is no longer being earned. People forget that, until very recently, they were struggling to establish themselves.

Before long, there comes to be a timeless quality to this phase, a sense of having arrived and a loss of concern about moving on. Like the Making It phase, this phase can last a very long time. And during most of that time there is little talk about further development. A few organizations—such as IBM—succeed in launching a renewal effort from this phase, and others (Hewlett-Packard comes to mind) try to do so. But if nothing is done to deflect the natural course of development, the Institution starts to close in on itself and lose its vital connection with the world.

6. Closing In

This phase often grows almost imperceptibly out of the self-satisfaction that so often marks institutional life. In an earlier time, when external competition was not as sharp in some fields as it is today (banking, for instance), this inward turning could produce a rather attractive "aristocratic" stylization of effort. The professional cultures of some fields—medicine and education are examples—serve as built-in justifications for Closing In when the organization gets to this point in its life cycle. If the organization is a governmental body that doesn't need to achieve success in the marketplace, the result is likely to be an increasingly unresponsive bureaucracy. If its market is competitive, however—and what markets are not competitive today?—the result is difficult to sustain. Employees forget the customers and focus on internal matters in a way that can seem almost perverse; they argue about rules and status while the whole operation is slowly collapsing. Whatever the external situation is and however quickly the organization is undermined, the Closing In phase marks the loss of the vital tension between the organization and its environment. Although it can be kept alive for some time by a "life-support system" of extraordinary assets or a monopolistic position, the natural and final outcome of closing in is—

Whoever in middle age, attempts to realize the wishes and hopes of his early youth invariably deceives himself. Each ten years of a man's life has its own fortunes, its own hopes, its own desires.

WOLFGANG VON GOETHE, GERMAN PHILOSOPHER

7. Dying

Unlike individuals, for whom dying is an event that can be pinned to a specific situation and date, organizations tend to come to the end of their lives in ways that make the fact of death less obvious. They get acquired, pieces of them are split off and sold, and it becomes harder and harder to say just when "the organization" ceased to exist. At this stage, organizations may go into Chapter 11 bankruptcy and then reemerge to function in a brief burst of energy, like a dying star, before darkness overtakes them. Even if they operate for a time, with skeleton staffs in little offices over a warehouse somewhere at the edge of the city, they come sooner or later to the point where the activities and the identity that once were that organization no longer exist. They have reached the end of the life cycle.

> *If we want things to stay as they are, things will have to change.*
>
> GIUSEPPE DI LAMPEDUSA,
> ITALIAN NOVELIST

The Role of Transition in the Organizational Life Cycle

Transitions are the dynamic interludes between one of the seven stages of organizational life and the next. Their function is to close out one phase, reorient and renew people in that time we are calling the neutral zone, and carry people into the new way of doing and being that is the beginning of the next stage. A single transition may not be enough to bring about the complete transformation of the organization and the reorientation of its people; there may instead be a string of transitions, each of which carries the organization a step further along the path of its development. These multi-transition turnings can take years to finish. But however long they take, they make sense to people only in the context of the organization's development. And transitions will need to make sense to people, for otherwise people will resist them and make it far harder for the organization to grow as it must.[6]

What is called "innovation" usually represents a new Dream. Mini-mills, which reprocess scrap into new steel, began as such a dream. Existing steel companies held fast to the more expensive and difficult process of making the metal directly out of ore, so for the dream to survive, it had to do so outside of existing organizations. The same thing happened with the dream of using transistors in radios instead of vacuum tubes. The big American electronics companies that were successful using vacuum tubes refused to embrace the new technology, and that dream was left to the Japanese to nurture. Looking at each of these cases as simply "innovation" underestimates the challenge they faced. What innovation's champions are actually doing is creating a new organization, and to do that they must go back to the start of the life cycle. What we call "an innovation" is really a new Dream.

The organizational world is full of leaders with big dreams, but to convert Dreams into Ventures, leaders have to go through a transition; many of them are not ready to do that. They have to let go of the perfect ideal or the effortless vision that the Dream represented and begin the hard work and the compromises that it takes to launch the Venture. Some who let themselves be pulled into that transition—often with grave misgivings—never manage to emerge from it. Years later they reminisce ineffectually about "the days when we sat around Charlie's office and talked about the whiz-bang new computer [or the knockout training program or the world-class consulting firm] that we could create." They remain wholeheartedly committed to the Dream, but they have found a dozen reasons why they cannot and should not go through the ending that will be necessary if they are to make the transition into the second age of organizational life, turning the Dream into the Venture.

Not everyone finds the transition from the Dream to the Venture so difficult of course, for fortunately there are people who are not as interested in the Dream as they are in creating an actual organization based upon it. They may not really feel comfortable, in fact, with the naked idea. They'd much prefer to have an office and a phone, an ad in the paper, and an actual product to deliver to a real, live customer. They are ready to start an actual company.

The Laws of Organizational Development

Even at this early point in the organizational life cycle, the First Law of Organizational Development is evident: *those who were most at home with the necessary activities and arrangements of one phase are the ones who are the most likely to experience the subsequent phase as a severe personal setback.* They will talk about it as a "strategic mistake," as "dumb," "unnecessary," and "too expensive." They will try to debate it on any other terms they can think of, but what they are really saying is that the transition is forcing them to let go of what they find most meaningful about the undertaking. And those who are well adapted and adjusted to the Venture will say the same things about the next stage, Getting Organized. In each of these cases, people who do not want to go through a transition will object to the change that caused it.

There is no fruit which is not bitter before it is ripe.

Publilius Syrus,
Latin writer

The Venture stage was exemplified by Hewlett-Packard in the late 1930s, by Apple Computer in the early 1980s, by AOL in the 1990s, and by thousands of lesser endeavors in between. The organization does fine for a while in a literal or figurative garage with a handful of people who are caught up in the founders' enthusiasm. Roles and routines are vague, and the only thing that matters is to get problems solved whenever and wherever they present themselves. Oh, yes, and the other rule: the worst mistake is to miss an opportunity.

The Venture stage demands entrepreneurial hustle. How things are done doesn't matter much, for in the crisis-driven atmosphere of most ventures, energy, commitment, the ability to interest others in the undertaking, and a pragmatic, flexible approach are more important than careful plans and tested systems. Although there isn't likely to be much hierarchy in the Venture stage, there is also not much doubt about who has the power. The values are those of the founders, and their personalities define the style of the whole organization. There is no formal decisionmaking process. The founders decide—or tell someone else to decide. The kind of people who cluster around such founders tend to be comfortable with someone else calling the shots, and they are likely to admire and idealize the founders. Loyalty is personal.

One must be thrust out of a finished cycle in life, and that leap [is] the most difficult to make— to part with one's faith, one's love, when one would prefer to renew the faith and recreate the passion.

ANAÏS NIN, AMERICAN DIARIST

As noted earlier, a Venture can last for a long time. But as it grows the people who are best fitted to its needs are likely to become somewhat ambivalent about its success. The success is what they have been trying to create, and it validates their efforts. But success leads to growth—and especially to increasing complexity—that cannot be contained within and rationalized by the old forms and the old outlook. As the Venture becomes less and less able to manage its own success and Getting Organized becomes more and more obviously necessary, we encounter the Second Law of Organizational Development: *the successful outcome of any phase of organizational development triggers its demise by creating challenges that it is not equipped to handle.*

The sequence of Dream-to-Venture-to-Getting-Organized is the growth pattern coded into the very DNA of organizational life, but an understanding of the transitions that the sequence requires is not. What you find in a young organization that is trying to get organized is chaos. Most of what made the original core group of employees valuable to the Venture makes them detrimental to the process of Getting Organized. The founder may be one of those assets-turned-liability. The disorganized creativity now blocks plans to bring out a commercially viable product. And the founder's intuitive way of following opportunities where and when they arise—which, he keeps reminding you, successfully guided the original research and brought in the original funding—is now a huge handicap to the management team, who are now starting to wish they could marginalize the founder.

So we get the Third Law of Organizational Development: *in any significant transition, the thing that the organization needs to let go of is the very thing that got it this far.* Discovering that law is painful, especially when you feel that you owe everything to the people, the culture, the style of management, or the strategy that "got you this far." And especially when people start saying: "I've given my life to making this little company successful, and now you tell me that you don't need my skills anymore! The organization has 'outgrown' me, you say? Well, I think that the truth is that you have no gratitude . . . no integrity . . . no decency . . . etc. . . . etc."

Such conflicts are reminders of the Fourth Law of Organizational Development: *whenever there is a painful, troubled time in the organization, a developmental transition is probably going on.* The terrible morale, the intragroup conflicts, or the sudden drop in productivity that you're trying to deal with are just symptoms of that transition and the toll it is taking on people. If such troubles are very disruptive, you may try to avoid making the transition. Yet if you do that, you will run into the Fifth Law of Organizational Development: *during the first half of the life cycle—through the Making-It stage—not to make a transition when the time is ripe for one to occur will cause a developmental "retardation" in the organization.* Numerical growth may continue for a time, but the conditions for further *development* will have been aborted by your avoidance of the transition, and in the end the retardation will threaten the very existence of the organization.

There is thus what we might call a "developmental imperative" that drives a company or an institution through the phases of the first half of the organizational life cycle. But after an organization has passed that point, things change. At first, there are few signs that Becoming an Institution is anything more than the next step onward and upward. But gradually people start to notice that form is becoming more important than function. Communication ceases to be a way to get through to others and begins to become a way to demonstrate an acceptable style and manner. People grow less and less likely to communicate directly with those who need to know and more likely to "go through channels"—and to complain when others do not. Efforts that involve doing anything differently are paced very slowly in the hope that doing things gradually will help to "bring everyone on board." In the institutional phase of their existence, organizations become so concerned with the stability of their

The important thing is this: to be able at any moment to sacrifice what we are for what we would become.

CHARLES DU BOS,
FRENCH CRITIC

own practices and the sanctity of their values that they end up generating the very problems that initiate the transition to the next phase of organizational life: Closing In.

Typically, the crises that bring institutionality to an end and initiate the transition to Closing In are external threats to market position or financial stability, brought on (be it noted) by the behaviors that are the downside of institutionality. Under these external challenges, the institutional concern for rules and policy becomes an obsession with showing that everything has been done properly and that expecting anything other than the unhappy outcome that actually occurred is in itself improper. The emphasis on following the proper channels turns the organization into a warren of organizational tunnels into which requests disappear and from which results and answers never emerge.

Most of the organizations we call bureaucracies are in this phase of their life cycle, but actually there are bureaucratic elements in any complex undertaking that is past the Getting Organized stage. So it is important to remember that the most telling signs of being Closed In are not just that routine squeezes out creativity and even efficiency—though these are actual outcomes. The real hallmark of Closing In is that the organization seals itself off from effective communication with its environment and becomes preoccupied with its own inner workings to the point where operations are ritualized into secret and magical acts.

Let me illustrate the behavior of a Closed In organization with the story of how the U.S. Navy handled the idea of "continuous-aim firing" a century ago.[7] Around 1900 an American naval officer named Sims discovered that British sailors had developed a way to compensate for the roll of a ship and to hold steady the barrel of a shipboard cannon that would otherwise be tilting up and down with the action of the waves. He was able to demonstrate that British warships, using the new system, were dozens of times more accurate than their American counterparts. He showed too that instead of having to time the firing to moments of relative stability between rolls, British naval gunners could aim and fire continuously.

Sims sent off his findings to the U.S. Bureau of Ordinance and the U.S. Bureau of Navigation, and he waited. And waited. It was only after he began circulating his reports through unofficial channels, in a fashion that his superiors felt to be "improper," that he even received a reply. Which was essentially this:

1. Our equipment is as good as that of the British, so the difference must be in the training of the gunners.

2. The training of gunners is not the responsibility of the bureau you have contacted but of the officers of the ships in question.

3. Therefore, and most importantly, "continuous-aim firing is impossible."

In a final and completely shocking demonstration of "impropriety," Sims broke through the evasions and denial by communicating directly with President Theodore Roosevelt. TR recalled Sims from the unofficial exile in China to which he had been banished by the navy top brass and appointed him inspector of target practice, a post in which he was able to demonstrate the effectiveness of the new techniques. The naval historian Elting Morison described the results. In tests conducted three years before Sims took over the gunnery post,

> five ships of the North Atlantic Squadron [had] fired five minutes each at a lightship hulk at the conventional range of 1,600 yards [just under a mile]. After 25 minutes of banging away, two hits had been made on the sails of the elderly vessel. Six years later [i.e., three years into the new Sims system] one naval gunner made 15 hits in one minute at a target 75x25 feet at the same range; half of them hit in a bull's eye 50 inches square.[8]

This is more than simply "one of those cases of resistance to change." It is an example of the normal behavior that one finds in an organization in the Closed In phase of its existence.

Organizational Renewal

Failing to understand the developmental course of organizational life not only confuses issues like the mature organization's resistance to innovation but mistakenly suggests that these issues are simply "problems" to be fixed rather than the normal behavior of a stage in the life of the organization. What such an organization needs is not fixing but renewal. Renewal comes about not by changing specific practices or cultural values but by taking the organization back to the start of its life cycle. Renewal—or the recovery of the youthful vigor that

There is no great invention, from fire to flying, which has not been hailed as an insult to some god.

J. B. S Haldane,
British scientist

the organization had earlier in its life cycle—is in fact wired right into the organizational life cycle. What you have to do is choose, not Closing In, but the Path of Renewal—as shown in this figure.

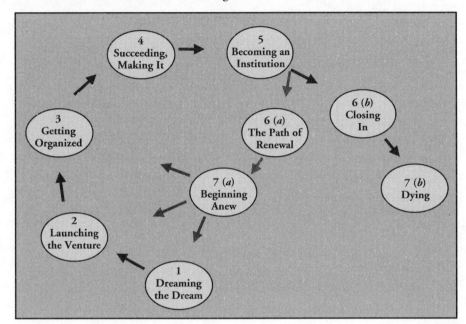

Figure 6.2   Organizational renewal.

To be sure, saying that you simply have to *choose* the right path makes it far simpler than the process of organizational renewal actually is. For the whole organizational "immune system" is set up to reject the results of making such a choice. Leaders who would go down this path must have a clear understanding of what they are doing and the resources to carry it off. But organizations as different as General Electric, the U.S. Army, and IBM show that it can be done, and that "old" organizations (well on their way to Dying) can in fact be rejuvenated.

As the figure suggests, renewal always involves finding ways to recapture and reincorporate the energy of the first three phases of the organizational life cycle.

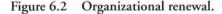

At every single moment of one's life, one is what one is going to be no less than what one has been.

OSCAR WILDE,
BRITISH DRAMATIST

1. *Redreaming the Dream:* Renewal must begin with Redreaming the Dream on which the organization is based. The new Dream might be the idea of becoming a service business (IBM) or reinventing the idea of leadership (the

U.S. Army). It might involve getting into entirely new business areas or simply redefining the organization's approach to existing ones. But in some significant way, organizational renewal always involves getting a new central idea around which to build the organization's activities and structures.

2. *Recapturing the Venture Spirit:* Next, the organization must Recapture the Venture Spirit; that style was natural to the young and just-launched organization, but now it is locked away in the past. This can be done with the help of new roles and structures (which properly belong to the third step of renewal). But the Venture Spirit is also more likely to be revived when a new cultural emphasis and style of leadership are encouraged, usually with the help of a new leadership development initiative. Anyone who would lead a renewal effort needs to behave like the founder of a new Venture—breaking down the walls between different functions, encouraging a looser and faster-moving decisionmaking process, and creating much closer linkages to customers.

3. *Getting Reorganized:* Renewal must also revisit the Getting Organized stage by remodeling the policies, roles, and structures of the organization to more nearly approximate those of a young organization. This time, of course, you are approaching Getting Organized from the other side, as it were, *recovering* the elements of successful organization rather than *developing* them from scratch. Sometimes this requires that you break up large units into smaller ones and treat the small units as little start-ups-within-the-company. You may need to reinvent the compensation system so that more of people's pay is tied directly to the results they achieve. You will probably need to move to a new and less qualification-bound kind of hiring, sacrificing certifications and formal experience for clear evidence that a job candidate can do the work that the organization currently needs to be done.

Needless to say, renewal puts any organization into a far-reaching state of transition. People who have grown used to the practices and culture of an Institution will have to let go of expectations and assumptions that have been rewarded for some time—expectations and assumptions, remember, that were natural to that phase and instrumental in getting the results that phase was designed to generate. These people are not flakes and slackers. Until things took an unexpected turn just recently, they were the organization's brightest and best.

Nothing is so dear as what you're about to leave.

JESSAMYN WEST,
AMERICAN WRITER

That is why transition is so difficult, and why it represents a crisis in an organization's life. It is a sudden and complete reversal in the trajectory that the organization has been following ever since its founding. That reversal is, to be sure, necessary if the organization is turn away from the path into terminal decline, but that fact does not make the necessary endings any easier for most people. It is important for leaders to comprehend the implications of what they are trying to achieve and not to let their understanding that renewal is essential blind them to the painful transitions that will be necessary to make things turn out as intended. It is also important for the HR and OD specialists who advise the leaders to recognize that transition management must be built into the very fabric of organizational renewal efforts.

And it is also important for these advisers to make sure their advice grows out of a real "developmental" context and represents a way to help the organization move along the natural path of its life cycle—or, if it is time, to reverse that direction and go back to make a fresh beginning with a formal renewal initiative. As we have said, a great deal of so-called organizational development has nothing whatsoever to do with *development* but is simply a technique for fixing a mechanical problem. Mechanical things, of course, do not *develop*. If your car is acting strangely, the mechanic doesn't say that he suspects it is "just going through a phase" or that "adolescent autos often have authority issues with their drivers." But an organization may indeed be going through a phase, for each of the developmental phases presents employees and leaders with predictable challenges. And the transitions between the phases present people with all of the difficulties that attend letting go, getting through the neutral zone, and making a new beginning.

Choosing the Path of Renewal

The natural cycle of organizational development, like other organic life cycles, carries a company or an institution through a sequence of stages that "unfold"—which is what "de-velop-ment" originally meant—out of an initial seed-dream as surely as an oak unfolds out of an acorn.

The first four stages represent "growth" in the positive meaning of that term. An organization that tries to skip one of them is headed for trouble, as is an organization that refuses to move on from one stage into the next one. But the fifth stage—Becoming an Institution—is different. It feels like a step forward to most people, although some may complain that the customer is starting to get overlooked and decisions are starting to take too long. But in time the downside of the institutional phase begins to cause more serious problems. It is then that farsighted leaders, with an instinctive sense of where things are headed, start to think about what it would take to revitalize the organization.

These leaders should start by asking themselves these three transition-based questions:

1. *What is it time for us to let go of?* No renewal can take place as long as people are holding on to the old ways of doing things and the old attitudes on which those ways are based. It's easier to identify what it's time for *others* to let go of; it's always harder to discern what it is time for *you* to let go of. Wise leaders, understanding that example is the most powerful tool they can employ, start with themselves: "What part of my identity—of the way I come across, and even the way I experience myself—do I need to let go of if we are going to enter the Path of Renewal?" Failing to ask (and of course answer) that question will result in one of those "this organization has to change!" initiatives that lead to so much chaos without actually changing anything inside the organization.

2. *How will we spend our time in the neutral zone?* The impatient leader is likely to want to Redream the Dream and Recapture the Venture Spirit and get the renewal-generating organizational infrastructure in place and working *tomorrow!* (Why wait when so much is riding on the outcome?) But you can't skip this "time in the wilderness." That neutral zone wilderness was where Moses's people discovered their renewal, remember? It's fine to get started with changes right away, but from the start you need to think of this as a long, complex process you are tackling. The transition is going to take months, at the least, and if the renewal involves a large, complex organization, it'll take years before it's complete. And most of the time will be spent in the neutral zone, so get comfortable there. How can you make others more comfortable there? What are the temporary rules and structures and resources that will make people's time in the neutral zone less anxiety-producing and more productive? At the very least, people are going to have to understand why they are in this crazy place and how they can get through it. (Remember the Four Ps? See pp. 60–69.)

3. *What is this new beginning going to require of us and of others in the organization?* The sooner you start embodying the behaviors and attitudes that

fit the new beginning, the sooner others in the organization will have the *leader* they need. But remember: in your communications you need to speak to wherever people are now, not to where you want them to go, and they need your help, not in getting to the destination you want them ultimately to reach, but in taking the next step in the transition they find themselves in because of your big change. What kind of reinforcements will really help people develop the new attitudes and behaviors that will be necessary if the beginning is to work?

Only in growth, reform, and change, paradoxically enough, is true security to be found.

ANNE MORROW
LINDBERGH,
AMERICAN WRITER

The transitions that mark the beginnings and endings of the stages of organizational life are not limited to corporations and institutions. They also govern the lives and developmental pathways of component units within organizations. A new regional office in a geographical area where there are emerging business opportunities begins as someone's Dream. A new project to develop a breakthrough product also begins as a Dream, as does a joint venture with a former competitor, a new cultural initiative, or a new governance structure. The organizational life cycle, with the seven phases we have described and the critical transition points between them, characterizes every one of these undertakings. They are different kinds of organizational undertaking, but they begin and develop in exactly the same way. Leaders need to understand that, and "leading" needs to be reconceived as the process by which a person helps some part of an organization—or the whole organization in the case of those at the top—to evolve along its developmental path by moving through a predictable sequence of organizational phases.

Conclusion

Transition is more than just the human side of change, the psychological process through which people go when a change occurs, or the way people reorient themselves to do things a new way. It is also the experience people have when an organization is moving from one stage of its development to the next. Often at such times no specific change has occurred to connect the transition to. All people know is that things "feel different" around the organization. As with the coming of a new season, the weather of everyday activity may slip back and forth for a while, and you may be unsure whether the new season is really at hand. But in a little while the early signals turn into unmistakable signs, and everyone can recognize that a significant change is at hand.

So it is with the end of one of the stages of the organizational life cycle. There's seldom any big, publicly visible change-event to serve as a marker—just a gradual end to "the way we used to do things." Under the pressure of new demands, things simply start to take on a new shape. Looking back, you will probably be able to say just when and how things changed. With the help of the material in this chapter, you'll also be able to say why change occurred. Time makes many things clear. Executive teams I have worked with can often, in hindsight, lay out a clear chronology of the stages of their organization's development and the events that triggered the transition from one stage to the next. But in the moment these same people found it very difficult to describe exactly what was happening.

The same ambiguity is usually present in the case of renewal. "Do we need it now? Have we reached the point where we are really 'closing in'?" That is why leaders need to learn all that they can about organizational development. It is their task to answer those questions—and to do so in the absence of definitive evidence. It is their task to make calls on developmental issues—and almost always, to do so on the basis of incomplete data. Unfortunately, there is no litmus test for whether an organization needs to be renewed, but it does help a great deal to know at what stage in the organizational life cycle a renewal is most likely to be needed and easiest to carry off. It helps to know the hallmarks of that developmental stage and to know that the transition that occurs at that point is disturbing to people. And it helps enormously to know how to manage the transition in a way that will help people move through the three phases of transition without undue distress. Then they will understand why they feel uncomfortable and won't take their frustrations out on the "stupid change" that is happening at the company.

Transition and Renewal: A Checklist

Yes   No

____ ____   Do I understand the seven stages of the organizational life cycle and how moving from one of them to the next puts an organization into transition?

____ ____   Can I identify where the organization I work in (or some other organization I know well) is in its own cycle of development?

____ ____   Can I distinguish between the details of my organization's current situation and its present stage of development?

__ __ Can I identify the original Dream that represented the first stage of my organization's life cycle?

__ __ Can I explain the characteristics of the Venture developmental stage and how they ultimately lead to the demise of that stage?

__ __ Do I understand the difference between everyday efforts to do things in a more organized way and the developmental stage called Getting Organized?

__ __ Can I explain the new concerns and attitudes that develop as an organization moves from Making It to Becoming an Institution?

__ __ Do I understand why Becoming an Institution represents a "moment of truth" for an organization—a time when it must make a critical choice that will determine whether the organization survives?

__ __ Can I explain this statement: "There is really nothing 'developmental' about most 'organizational development.' It's really just organizational 'repair.'"

__ __ Do I know the three transition-based questions to ask whenever I am trying to plan how the organization can move through one of the transformative times between one developmental phase and the next?

---

1. Adizes's article, which deserves to be better known, appeared originally in *Organizational Dynamics* (Summer 1979), pp. 3–25.

2. Parts of this chapter appeared as "Turning Points in the Organizational Life Cycle" in my book *Surviving Organizational Transition,* a book that was originally published in 1988 by Doubleday and is now available from William Bridges & Associates (visit www.wm.bridges.com for information). Other parts of the chapter appeared as the article "What's Developmental About Organizational Development?" in *Vision/Action: The Journal of the Bay Area Organizational Development Network* 6, no. 3 (March 1987), pp. 1–3.

3. For an elaboration of this argument, see my article "What's Developmental About Organizational Development?" (see note 2).

4. These "ages" draw on Adizes's writing, but they have been reshaped by two decades of my own work.

5. At one making-it organization where I was working with the executive team, I said, "At this point, the organization might decide it needed a bigger, more impressive boardroom—with a fine, big table!" Everyone began to laugh, and the CEO turned red. He had just had such a table installed.

6. Looking at the epigraph to this chapter, you will see that Adizes sees the importance of understanding the "different roles . . . [and] different organizational behavior" that will be required by the new phase in the organizational life cycle. He is talking about the situational *changes* that the organization is going to make, not the *transitions* that it is going to have to get its people through. That is very important, of course, but our concern here is different.

7. This story is recounted in Elting Morison, "Gunfire at Sea: Conflict over a New Technology," *Engineering and Science* (April 1950).

8. Ibid.

Part THREE

Dealing with Nonstop Change in the Organization and Your Life

Chapter Seven

How to Deal with Nonstop Change

There is one fault that I must find
With the twentieth century,
And I'll put it in a couple of words:
Too adventury.
What I'd like would be some nice dull monotony,
If anyone's gotony.
　　　　—Ogden Nash, American poet

It must be admitted that there is a degree of instability which is inconsistent
with civilization. But on the whole the great ages have been unstable ages.
　　　　—Alfred North Whitehead, British philosopher

It has become a truism that the only constant today is change. (Ironically, the Greek philosopher Heracleitus said the very same thing—2,500 years ago!) Yet we all feel that change is different today: it's continuous, wall-to-wall, nonstop. Our department is reorganized, and that's hardly finished when a new director arrives and decides to reorganize it again. Or just as everyone is recovering from the introduction of new database software, they announce that the whole distribution process is being outsourced. We talk not of *a single* change but of change as an ongoing phenomenon. It is a collage, not a simple image: one change overlaps with another, and it's all change as far as the eye can see.

That being so, what I've been saying about transition may seem artificial—like some kind of pure substance that can be isolated in the laboratory but never found in nature. In a sense, that's true. The image of transition I've been drawing is an ideal one. It's like those textbook diagrams of flowers or minerals that are more perfect than anything you'll ever encounter in the real world.

He has too many lice to feel an itch.

CHINESE PROVERB

The clarity of this ideal image of transition, however, is useful. Ironically, one of the reasons organizations have paid so little attention to transition is that they're overwhelmed by it. Transition is all around them—so close that they can't see it clearly. It's not until it's isolated in its simplest form that it can be seen clearly. Once you understand the pure and simple transitions I have been discussing, you can more easily understand the inner dynamics and outer effects of your own transitions. Fortunately, real transitions (like real daisies and real gold ore) look enough like their diagrammed counterparts to be recognizable. But that said, we now have to leave behind the image of the isolated transition and deal with the facts of a constantly changing environment.

The Three Phases

Overlap

In our conceptual picture of transition, there is an ending, then a neutral zone, and only then a new beginning. But those phases are not separate stages with clear boundaries. As the figure suggests, the three phases of transition are more like curving, slanting, overlapping strata than like sequential stages.

Each of these three processes starts before the preceding one is totally finished. That is why you are likely to be in more than one of these phases at the

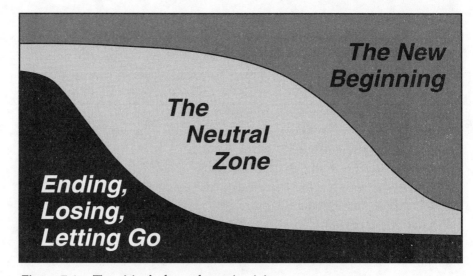

Figure 7.1   Transition's three phases (again).

same time and why the movement through transition is marked by a change in the *dominance* of one phase over the other two rather than an absolute shift from one to another.

Add the Fact of Simultaneous Changes

It gets even more complicated, for changes spin off from changes in a never-ending sequence. In the changeover to a new information management system, for example, you can be almost done (launching a new beginning) at the very same time that you are just entering the transition caused by a recently announced reorganization (letting go of the old structure). To make things harder, you are right in the middle of a neutral zone that opened up after last month's layoffs.

Your experience as a leader or a manager can be compared to that of someone conducting an orchestra: you have to keep track of the many different instruments, each playing different sequences of notes and each starting or stopping on its own terms. While you keep a sense of the whole piece, you have to shift your attention from one section to another. It is important for you to hold in your mind the overall design of the melody and harmonies, for unless you do that, every little change will sound like a new and unrelated melody that just happened to come along, without any relation to the rest of the music.

The first thing you're going to need in order to handle nonstop organizational change is *an overall design within which the various and separate changes are integrated as component elements.* In periods of major strategic change, such a design may have been announced to the organization by its leadership. When that happens, you're fortunate. Even if you don't entirely agree with the logic of the larger change, you benefit from the coherence it gives to the component changes.

If, on the other hand, no larger strategy exists, you'll need to analyze the changes and discover—or perhaps even invent—their underlying common purpose. These might include:

- The need to save money

- The need to recapture markets lost to a new competitor

- The need to respond creatively to a new climate of public opinion

- The need to speed up decisionmaking by decentralizing authority

Omnia uno tempore agenda. (Everything had to be done at once.)

JULIUS CAESAR DESCRIBING HOW HE HANDLED AN UNEXPECTED, SIMULTANEOUS ATTACK BY THE NERVII AT THREE DIFFERENT POINTS ON HIS FLANKS, WHILE PART OF HIS TROOPS WERE CROSSING A RIVER AND ANOTHER PART WERE SETTING UP CAMP

It may be helpful to think of your organization's history as a "life history" and to think of the present as the crossover point between one "chapter" and another of the history of that life. Imagine what you would entitle those two chapters, and the movement from the first to the second will probably give you a clearer picture of the overarching change that your organization is going through at present.

Whether you do it this way or in some other way, you have to find a few larger patterns that integrate and make sense out of all of the specific changes. (A client, recalling the childhood puzzles she liked, recently called it "connecting the dots and discovering the 'hidden object.'") When you've done that, you can use it to orchestrate your responses.

The Rising Tide of Change

You have one characteristic of human nature on your side, though it always seems to kick in a little too late to make any particular change easy. That is the human capacity, over time, to adjust to new and higher levels of change. If a group of eighteenth-century Europeans were transplanted to Wall Street or to downtown Tokyo, they would be completely overwhelmed by the number of changes in those places. But modern people are dealing with just such changes successfully every day—changes that only a couple of generations ago would have wiped people out.

The hardest thing to deal with is not the pace of change but *changes in the acceleration of that pace.* It is the acceleration of the pace of change in the past several decades that we are having trouble assimilating and that throws us into transition. Any change in the acceleration of change—even a deceleration— would do that: if change somehow suddenly ceased today, people would have difficulty because *the lack of change would itself be a change* and would throw them into transition.

He who sleeps in continual noise is wakened by silence.

WILLIAM DEAN HOWELLS, AMERICAN WRITER

This isn't just wordplay. As a start-up grows, develops, and ages, this kind of slowdown can actually take place as the company works to establish standardized policies and systems. As we saw in the last chapter, when it does that, many of the people who were happy with the old, chaotic status quo become unhappy with the new situation. They say things like, "The fun is gone," or, "This used to be a good company to work for," or, "We've turned into just another conventional company." (They might, if they were following the suggestion I made earlier, entitle the chapter that was ending, "Good-bye to Camelot" and the new chapter "Welcome to the Conventional World.")

Postpone "Extra" Changes

Even after you've clustered the changes under a few headings, you'll find that you have too many of them to manage effectively. You simply have to cut some of them out. Now, you can't keep the external world or other parts of your organization from affecting your part of the business, but you can often postpone or sometimes cancel incidental changes that are unrelated to the larger shift you have to deal with. The gains from those incidental changes are seldom large enough to compensate for their disruptive effects, and a crucial large change can be jeopardized when smaller changes are thoughtlessly piggybacked on top of it.

Two quite opposite qualities equally bias our minds—habit and novelty.

JEAN DE LA BRUYÈRE,
FRENCH WRITER

We sometimes think that because we're changing lots of things, we might as well change everything. But that only makes sense if "everything" is an interrelated whole. All too often, extra changes get added to the pile only because some leaders or managers have become personally "hooked" on change. They like the adrenalin rush of being immersed in a crisis situation, and in an environment where crises naturally abound they become habituated to it. Sometimes an extra change stirs things up and forces them to start over again just as the going gets rough, so it saves them from having to do the hard work of following through on a change that is already under way. Change-addicted leaders are dangerous people, although they may also be charismatic and can usually make a plausible-sounding case for whatever additional change they are proposing to make.

Foresee as Much as You Can

Economic and social forecasting is a big business, but when tested against subsequent events, it misses as many boats as it catches. John Naisbitt's *Megatrends*[1] and the megawave of books it launched are fascinating reading, and they address the natural human desire to know what the future holds. The trouble is that they have not managed to forecast events with very much accuracy.

Consider the stock pickers. Few of them even match what you could achieve yourself with random picks. Or think of all the "hot new products" that don't go anywhere. Each of those products was touted as a winner by professionals who were supposed to know. But most of the predictions were based on the forces that produced the circumstances of the present rather than the forces that would produce the future. Those who prepared for "change" in Eastern Europe in 1988 turned out to be ready for an extension of what was going on in 1980, not for the reality of the twenty-first century.

Those who base their plans on predictions are like the French who built an "impregnable" line of tank-proof fortifications before World War I, which they named for their minister of war, André Maginot, and around which the Germans did an end-run in World War II. They are like the companies that embraced the principle of vertical integration just in time to find that conglomeration was the hot new answer. (But by the time they got around to conglomeration, of course, the marketplace favored focus and filling niches. And now that everyone is finding a niche . . . well, you get the idea.)

There are two problems with forecasting. First, the relation between things is so immensely complex and the outcomes of that complexity are so unpredictable that it is almost impossible to know enough to say with any confidence what is going to happen. Second, forecast-based plans create a bandwagon effect that changes the conditions on which the forecasts themselves were based. Walter Macrae made the point very well in an article he wrote for *The Economist* almost 20 years ago:

> In modern conditions of high elasticity of both production and substitution, we will generally create temporary but large surpluses of whatever the majority of decision-influencing people five or ten years earlier believed was going to be in most desperately short supply. This is because the well-advertised views of the decision influencers tend to be believed by both the profit-seeking private producers and consensus-following governments, and these two then combine to cause excessive production of precisely the things that the decision influencers had been saying would be the most obviously needed.[2]

So, because everyone is trying to benefit from the predictions, they change their behavior—on which the predictions were based—and the predictions prove wrong.

Shallow men speak of the past; wise men of the present; and fools of the future.

MARQUISE DU DEFFAND, FRENCH EPIGRAMMATIST

I have seen the future, and it's a lot like the present, but much longer.

DAN QUISENBERRY, PROFESSIONAL BASEBALL PLAYER

There are two kinds of forecasting that *can* help you to be ready for change. Neither is so exciting as guessing the numbers that will be thrown on the political or economic dice, but both are more reliable. The first is to do life-cycle forecasts on the organizational policies and structures that you are currently utilizing. Such life-cycle planning is done regularly for products, for everyone knows that sooner or later technological change and competitive pressures will make today's successful product obsolete. So organizations begin, while the product is still high on the curve of its success, to plan for its modification or replacement.

In the same way, life-cycle planning should be done for levels of employment, for areas of technical expertise, and for cultural emphases. All have as clearly limited a life expectancy as does a product. Today's retirement package, for example, may be on its last legs, as may the supervisors' training program and the way the organization does its succession planning. Only a life-cycle-based approach to these issues will give you the lead time to avoid the predictable crisis of having to manage a big transition triggered by a change that no one foresaw. You may not be able to convince people that things that aren't "broke" yet still need fixing, but you can certainly be ready with alternatives when the first cracks are discovered.

Do Worst-Case Scenarios

A second way to be ready for the future is to build into every plan a "what if?" clause. What if the automation project takes twice as long as everyone says it will? What if 50% more people than you predicted take you up on the early retirement offer? (And what if they're the wrong people, the ones you want to keep?) What if a government regulation or a legal decision forces you to stop using a certain chemical? What if a 6.8 earthquake hits the manufacturing site or distribution center? In other words, what if things don't turn out the way you hope and plan that they will?

The only way to prepare for the unexpected is to build into all of your plans a contingency clause that suggests what you would do if the unexpected happened. In that way you will have alternative routes ready to take if the main route is closed unexpectedly, as well as established procedures for changing your plans with a minimum of chaos if they are undermined by unforeseen events. There is a further advantage to worst-case scenarios: if everyone else, as the Macrae quotation suggests, is going the way you were planning to, the worst-case scenario becomes a forecast that may be accurate simply because it is based on something other than commonly accepted assumptions. "Contrarian" investment strategies are based on precisely this approach.

Make the Transition to "Change as the Norm"

Getting people to deal effectively with nonstop change demands that they develop a new mindset. And in most organizations, doing that requires a very significant transition: old assumptions and expectations have to be relinquished, and a long, difficult journey made through the neutral zone, before any viable new beginning is even in sight. It isn't enough to preach about the Promised Land by describing the benefits of "continuous improvement" or "thriving on chaos." It isn't even enough to inspire people with vignettes of companies that are said to be doing these things. You have to manage the big transition from the old assumptions and expectations of isolated and piecemeal change to the new ones of continuous change.

Stability itself is nothing else than a more sluggish motion.

MICHEL DE MONTAIGNE, FRENCH PHILOSOPHER

That task is no different from managing any other big transition, and the preceding three chapters should provide the tactics you need. My point is that nonstop change is simply a lot of different changes that overlap each other—as changes have always done—as well as an increase in the rate of overlapping change. Every new level of change is termed "nonstop" by people who are having trouble with transition.

At the same time, every previous level of change comes to be called "stability." Seen in this light, what people today call "nonstop change" is simply a new level of what has always existed. It isn't pure chaos—simply a new experience. When people adjust to it, they will look back upon it as "the stability that we used to enjoy."

This is more than a simple argument about the meanings of words. In companies that have successfully institutionalized the practice of "continuous improvement," procedures are constantly being changed to increase productivity, maximize efficiency, and reduce costs. Little transitions are going on all the time. Without some larger, overarching continuity, everyone's world would feel like chaos. But what does not change in even the most constantly evolving environment is the expectation that every status quo is just a temporary expedient until a better way to do things has been discovered. Every one of those little improvements, though it may cause transitions, reaffirms the unchanging values and procedures that underlie "continuous improvement."

Not all changes are improvements, of course. Some are simply small readjustments to maintain the present balance. Some are larger moves to cut losses or to repair damage done by market changes and regulatory actions. The point, however, remains the same: only if continuous change is normalized as the new status quo can it be assimilated. People have to understand that the point of change is to preserve that which does not change. The continuation of anything depends on its changing, just as staying upright and traveling straight ahead on a bicycle depends on making constant steering adjustments. Refusing to make those little changes would not produce "stability" but, on the contrary, would rapidly lead to the loss of balance and motion.

Progress, far from consisting in change, depends on retentiveness. When change is absolute there remains no being to improve and no direction is set for possible improvement. . . . When experience is not retained . . . infancy is perpetual.

GEORGE SANTAYANA,
AMERICAN PHILOSOPHER

Clarify Your Purpose

Stability through change demands clarity about who you are and what you are trying to do. That is the starting point, because there must be something to adjust before there can be an adjustment. Times of continuous change, like our world today, put a premium on knowing clearly what you are trying to accomplish. Whether it be a small team of hourly workers or a multinational corporation, what is the purpose of the unit that you manage?

The answer to this question does not lie in high-sounding words like those company philosophies you see over people's desks. The answer lies in whether people have a clear sense of how their activities contribute to the larger whole. An organization's purpose is seldom tricky: Toyota's purpose is to build cars and related vehicles; Harvard University's purpose is to educate people and push back the boundaries of knowledge; your community hospital's purpose is to provide medical care and treatment that cannot be given at home or in a doctor's office. Every component part of any large organization has its own purpose that in some way makes the overall purpose possible. (If it doesn't, that part has come unplugged from the whole and its existence is no longer justified.)

Far too many organizational purpose statements are really descriptions of the organization's objectives: to increase shareholder value, to give customers their money's worth, to be a good place to work. These are very important goals to work toward, but they aren't the strategic threads that everyday

Many are stubborn in pursuit of the path they have chosen, few in pursuit of the goal.

FRIEDRICH NIETZSCHE,
GERMAN PHILOSOPHER

changes are meant to preserve. It is the purpose, not the objectives, that is the heartbeat of the organization.

The confusion of purposes and objectives has serious repercussions in a time when change is the norm. Sometimes an organization has to make changes in its objectives to preserve its purpose:

The company whose purpose is to produce the best possible containers switches from manufacturing glass bottles to plastic ones.

The company whose purpose is to create high-quality preserved food shifts from canning to freezing.

The company whose purpose is to provide people with a way to transport packages quickly sells its railcars and buys a fleet of airplanes.

Any of these changes would put a corporation into transition, but all of them were undertaken to ensure a continuity of purpose. The same is true on every organizational level, down to the team level, where people share a much more specific collective purpose. New machinery is introduced to carry out that purpose more effectively. So is the new organizational design or the new policy or the new emphasis on quality or customer service.

The trouble is that people come to identify with the objectives rather than the purpose. They do so because it is easier to relate their own efforts and their own self-image to the objective, which is more tangible and closer at hand, than to the purpose. Thus, you must work constantly to get people to identify with the organization's purpose. That takes explanation, modeling, and reward.

> *Management by objectives works if you know the objectives. Ninety percent of the time you don't.*
>
> PETER DRUCKER,
> AMERICAN MANAGEMENT
> EXPERT

Rebuild Trust

If you have ever watched people learning to swim, you'll remember that critical moment when they pushed off from the edge of the pool and set forth on their own. You may have heard the swimming teacher say, at such a time, "I won't let you sink." Without trust in the teacher, that step toward independence and the mastery of a new skill would have been less likely to happen. At that moment, with fear balanced against hope, it is trust that makes the difference. Not yet trusting their own ability to swim, they fall back on trusting the teacher.

It's much the same with transition management. When people trust their manager, they're willing to undertake a change even if it scares them. When they don't feel that trust, transition is much less likely to occur. The good news is that you can build such trust; the bad news is that it takes time to build trust—so it behooves you to get started right away.

There are two sides to trust: the first is outward-looking and grows from a person's past experiences with that particular person or group; the second is inward-looking and comes from the person's own history, particularly from childhood experiences. The level of trust that anyone feels is fed by both of these sources. You have control over the outward-facing source, so start there. The technique is simple—simple to explain anyway: *start being trustworthy.*

Trustworthiness is encouraged by a number of actions that are within your power to take:

1. Do what you say you will do. Don't make promises you can't or won't keep. Most people's mistrust has come from the untrustworthy actions of others in the past.

2. If for any reason you cannot follow through on a promise, warn the person as soon as the situation becomes clear to you, and explain the circumstances that led to your failure to do what you promised.

3. Listen to people carefully and tell them what you think they are saying. If you have it wrong, accept the correction and revise what you say. People trust most the people whom they believe understand them.

4. Understand what matters to people and work hard to protect anything that is related to what matters to them. People trust those who are looking out for their best interests.

5. Share yourself honestly.[3] A lot of mistrust begins when people are unable to read you. And remember: while hiding your shortcomings may polish your image, it ultimately undermines people's trust in you. Admitting an untrustworthy action is itself a trustworthy action.

6. Ask for feedback and acknowledge unasked-for feedback on the subject of your own trustworthiness whenever it is given. Regard it as valuable information and reflect on it. Feedback may be biased, and you don't have to swallow it whole. But check it for important half-truths.

If you tell the truth, you don't have to remember anything.

Mark Twain,
American writer

He who mistrusts most should be trusted least.

THEOGNIS OF MEGARA,
GREEK POET

7. Don't try to push others to trust you further than you trust them. You will communicate subtly whatever mistrust you are feeling, and it will be returned to you in kind. Trust is mutual, or else it is very shallow.

8. Try extending your trust of others a little further than you normally would. Being trusted makes a person more trustworthy, and trustworthy people are more trusting.

9. Don't confuse being trustworthy with "being a buddy." Being a buddy for any purpose besides friendship is an *untrustworthy* act. Besides, trust doesn't automatically come with friendship.

10. Don't be surprised if your trust-building project is viewed suspiciously. Asking people to let go of their old mistrust of managers (and of you in particular) puts them into a significant (and dangerous-feeling) transition. Their mistrust—justified or not—was a form of self-protection, and no one gives up self-protection easily.

11. If all of this is too complicated to remember and you want a single key to the building of trust, just remind yourself, "Tell the truth."

As to what you can do with the inner face of mistrust—which goes back to people's childhoods—the same advice holds true. The difference is that if a person's history has reinforced their mistrust of others, you will make even slower headway than you will in combating the mistrust you've earned by your own actions. But you *can* make headway with even the most mistrustful person, so get started. Every hour that mistrust continues makes transition more difficult to manage than it has to be.

Unload Old Baggage

Managers sometimes find themselves fighting old battles when transition starts. These battles may even precede the manager's own tenure—the layoff back in '73 that was handled so badly; the promise about seniority rights that wasn't kept when the contract was renegotiated; the repeated statements three years ago that the plant wouldn't be closed (but it was).

At times like this you feel like yelling, "You're not going to bring *that* up again, are you?" or, "You're not blaming *me* for that, are you?" The answer, of course, is "Yes." Transition is like a low-pressure area on the organizational weather map. It attracts all the storms and conflicts in the area, past as well as present. This is because transition "decompresses" an organization. Many of the barriers that held things in check come down. Old grievances resurface. Old scars start to ache. Old skeletons come tumbling out of closets.

In the short run, this can complicate an already complicated situation. But in the longer run it can have a positive impact. Every transition is an opportunity to heal the old wounds that have been undermining effectiveness and productivity. If leaders have lied in the past, this is the time to tell the truth and rebuild credibility on the basis of honesty. If people have been terminated callously in the past, this is the time to terminate people with dignity and fairness and start building the values of concern and respect for employees in general. If employee concerns have been disregarded in the past, this is a time to begin listening. It is never too late to become an organization that manages its people well. For that reason, the old scar and the unresolved issue are great gifts. They represent opportunities for organizational enhancement.

Sell Problems, Not Solutions

As I said in chapter 3, people let go of outlived arrangements and bygone values more readily if they are convinced that there is a serious problem that demands a solution. But the idea of selling problems is more than just a practical tactic to encourage people to let go of the way things have been. In an organization in which change is the norm, selling problems is the only way to get beyond having to sell every change piecemeal. Here are some of the ways in which selling problems contributes to your ability to manage nonstop change successfully:

1. People who understand the organization's real problems are in the market for solutions and don't have to be "informed" or "educated" after the fact. When things are changing very fast, often there isn't time to do that.

2. If you understand the problem and the people you work with don't, a polarity is immediately set up. If, on the other hand, everyone recognizes the importance of the same problem, it's the manager and people on one side and the problem on the other. Only with such cooperation can organizations respond quickly to the challenges they encounter.

3. If everyone recognizes the problem, it is likely to be solved much faster. Whatever solution is selected is more likely to meet everyone's needs because those needs were clear during the problem-solving stage. Any solution that doesn't take people's needs into account will never sell.

4. Finally, selling problems implicates everyone in the solution. It says, in effect, "If you want to be part of the solution, get involved. If you don't, don't complain."

In light of these points, it is ironic that involving people is sometimes viewed as too time-consuming for a world of rapid change. Actually, it is the authoritarian style and the command mentality that goes with it that take too much time—time spent slugging it out to overcome each pocket of self-interest, trying to motivate people who feel that the change was forced on them, arguing with people who don't even know that there are problems. Selling problems is, in fact, the investment that pays long-term dividends by making people readier for particular organizational transitions—and for a world of continuous change in general.

Another Key to Managing Nonstop Change: "Challenge and Response"

We are constantly hearing about *competitiveness, game plans,* and *winning.* In a society as sports-minded as ours, those terms strike a ready chord—the more so when we seem to be falling behind in a game in which we were once the dominant player. But the sports metaphor is dangerously misleading. It suggests that there is a coherent *game* going on, and that the *winners* will come out ahead because they *beat their opponents.* It suggests that they win because they are a better *team,* with better talent, training, and strategy.

In fact, there are no final scores in the world of nonstop change. What we call "victory" is actually just being ahead in the early innings of a game. Besides, real success goes not to the organizations that set out to beat the opposition, but to the organizations that focus on the environment as a whole rather than on the competition. We are in one of those periods of evolutionary shift, and becoming preoccupied with the competition is shortsighted. *It is not by competing but by capitalizing on the rapid pace of change that today's organiza-*

tions will thrive. And that is as true of a department or a project team as it is of organizations as a whole.

There are a couple of keys to capitalizing on change. One lies in understanding and utilizing "the cycle of challenge and response." As historian Arnold J. Toynbee demonstrated in his book *A Study of History,* the great civilizations have risen to power not because of their advantages, but because they treated their disadvantages as *challenges* to which they discovered creative *responses.*

Toynbee shows, for example, that ancient Athens rose to dominance in the classical world after its soil was depleted. Instead of being destroyed by what was a huge setback for an agricultural country, the Athenians treated their problem as a challenge to find a new way to participate actively in the economy of their day. Their creative response was to turn to the cultivation of olives, which draw on a deeper water table than do field crops. The Athenians rebuilt their economy around the export of olive oil—which further challenged them to build a merchant marine to transport the oil, a pottery industry to build the amphoras to contain the oil during shipment, and a mining industry to create the coin to pay for all the peripheral transactions of such trade. New responses thus created new challenges in another part of the society or the economy.[4]

Descending from the serious to the comic, the contemporary television sitcom grew out of the original *I Love Lucy* show, which was itself a response to a challenge that might have doomed a less "responsive" crew. Lucille Ball and Desi Arnaz didn't want to live in New York City, where the TV comedies of their day were filmed and from which they were broadcast to relay stations around the country. Instead, they decided to film the show on 35-millimeter film in Los Angeles and distribute the show like a movie through CBS affiliates. Not only did their response work, but it also changed network distribution patterns and (for better or worse) created the possibility of TV reruns, because the movie film kept its quality much longer than did the kinescopes that were then being used to record TV shows.

The point of these examples is not that you can forget about the competition. It is simply that your competition is the critical factor only when the game (to use the favorite competitive metaphor) is not changing very significantly. When a business or industry is going through a profound transformation—and there aren't any that I know of today that are not—focusing on competition blinds you to the real challenge, which is *capitalizing on change.* Competing for market share in today's markets is too much like fighting for deck chairs on the *Titanic.*

For the manager there is another advantage to the challenge and response approach to dealing with change: it can be used at any level of the organization. Start at the top: an organization's leaders face challenges, and they come up with responses, which might be to launch a new product or go after a new kind of customer. Such responses, in turn,

> provide upper-level managers with *their* challenge: How do we redefine the purposes and even the identities of our units in light of this new organizational direction? Whatever it is, that group's response

> provides middle managers with *their* challenge: How do we reorganize our efforts to serve the new unit purpose? And the middle managers' creative responses to that question represent a

> challenge to supervisors to come up with new responses at the team level, which in turn

> challenge individual workers to respond creatively at the point where the product is made or the service is delivered.

This cascading of challenge and response breaks the stranglehold of passivity that develops when managers, supervisors, and workers see their jobs as merely carrying out the orders of those above them. In a world characterized by nonstop change, every level of the organization must see its situation as a challenge calling not for compliance but for creative response. When that happens, people are no longer mere victims who must wait and see what others decide—and then act unquestioningly. Challenge and response restores a sense of control and purpose to people, no matter at what level of the organization they work.

And, incidentally, it knocks the socks off the competition, just the way it did more than 2,000 years ago in Athens.

The Final Key: Increasing the Organization's Transition-Worthiness

Sometimes when I run transition management workshops for organizations, I ask people to rearrange themselves in a circle by birthday and then use their new configuration to divide up into small working groups. Two things become evident when I do this. First, the people can watch themselves individually and the group as a whole going through transition—letting go of their old locations, milling around in a chaotic neutral zone, and finding a new location for themselves. It also provides them with a firsthand experience of what each phase of the process feels like.

Second, they can see how the size of the group and the arrangement of the particular room we're meeting in affects how easy or hard it is to relocate in it. If there are fixed chairs (as in an auditorium) it takes forever for people to make their way from one location to another. If the walls are very close to the seating, the relocation is also slowed down. And because of its more complicated dynamics, a very big group takes much longer to reconfigure itself than a small group.

Having seen this, people are in a better position to describe the conditions within an organization that may make it more difficult to get people through a transition. People who have held narrowly defined jobs for a long time are sure to have a hard time with reorganizations that involve redefining those jobs. People who have little contact with people working elsewhere in the organization have trouble too. Certain policies and procedures make life difficult for people in transition, while other policies and resources—a relocation program or a practice of periodic reassignments or a wide use of cross-functional teams—can make the experience of transition less confusing and disruptive.

Boats are termed "seaworthy" if their construction keeps them afloat, even under challenging conditions, or "unseaworthy" if their construction doesn't do so. By analogy, organizations can be said to be "transition-worthy" or "un-transition-worthy"—their policies, structure, roles, resources, culture, histories, and leadership are either helping or hindering their ability to manage transition.

Stated so generally, that sounds a little esoteric. But if you ask people who work for your organization which conditions and arrangements within the organization are helping and which are hindering their ability to let go of the old, live with a confusing time in the neutral zone, and make a solid new beginning, they can tell you. Listen to them. And do whatever you can to make the organization more transition-worthy. It'll pay off, because one thing about nonstop change is . . . it doesn't stop. It is a problem that won't go away.

Managing in a World of Nonstop Change: A Checklist

Yes   No

___ ___ Have I accepted the fact that nonstop change is the unavoidable reality today, or am I still fighting it?

___ ___ Am I orchestrating my transition management tactics effectively, shifting from change situation to change situation, and from an ending here to a beginning there?

___ ___ Do I have an overall mental picture in which this particular transition makes sense?

___ ___ If I do not have such a picture, am I working to create one for myself and my people by "connecting the dots" or identifying the particular "end of a chapter" that we may be facing?

___ ___ Am I being careful not to introduce extra, unrelated changes while my people are still struggling to deal with the big transitions?

___ ___ Am I watching out that I don't stake too much on a particular future that someone is forecasting?

___ ___ Am I making (and asking others to make) life-cycle projections to identify and start creating replacements for policies, systems, and structures that have passed their midlife points?

___ ___ Do I include worst-case scenarios in my change management plans, both for their own sake and as "contrarian" planning?

___ ___ Am I planning and managing the transition from "occasional change" to "change as the norm" and encouraging others to do the same?

___ ___ Do I honestly think of the status quo as a temporary and expedient resting place in a time of constant change?

___ ___ Do I talk of change as the best way to preserve the essential continuity of the organization?

___ ___ Have I clarified the purpose of my organization and helped others under me to do the same for their level of the organization?

___ ___ Are these purposes distinguished from the objectives that different groups are trying to reach?

___ ___ Do I have a deep feeling for this purpose, or am I merely mouthing words?

___ ___ Have I worked hard to unpack old baggage, heal old wounds, and finish unfinished business?

___ ___ Do I regularly work to sell the organization's problems?

___ ___ Do I look at my own organizational environment as a challenge demanding a creative response, and do I encourage others to do the same?

___ ___ Am I gathering information—particularly in the aftermath of a big change—about what helped and what hindered people in making their transitions? And am I using it to make the organization's policies, structure, roles, resources, and culture more transition-worthy?

Am I actively working to rebuild trust in the following ways:

___ ___ 1. Being very careful to do what I say I will do?

___ ___ 2. Listening to people carefully and letting them know what I hear them saying?

___ ___ 3. Understanding what matters to people and working hard to protect whatever is related to that?

___ ___ 4. Sharing myself honestly (without letting honesty be a cover for hostility)?

___ ___ 5. Asking for feedback and acknowledging unasked-for feedback on the subject of my own trustworthiness?

___ ___ 6. Remembering not to push others to trust me further than I trust them?

___ ___ 7. Trying to extend my trust of others a little further?

___ ___   8. Not confusing being trustworthy with "being a buddy"?

___ ___   9. Not being surprised if my trust-building project is viewed a bit suspiciously?

___ ___   10. Constantly reminding myself to tell the truth?

Final Questions

What actions could you take to help people deal more successfully with the nonstop change in which your organization currently finds itself and become more able to do so in the future? What could you do today to get started on these tasks? (Write yourself a memo in the space below.)

---

1. John Naisbitt, *Megatrends: Ten New Directions Transforming Our Lives* (New York: Warner Books, 1983).

2. Walter Macrae, "The Coming Entrepreneurial Revolution," *The Economist,* November 25, 1976.

3. One warning, though: don't let honesty become a cover and an excuse for hostility. This kind of honesty will destroy trust just as fast as dishonesty will.

4. As this example shows, I am talking here about "challenges" in a very serious sense. I work with many organizations that regularly use "challenges" as a verbal way to put a positive spin on—and to keep them from having to say—"problems." An organization that doesn't like to talk about its problems is very seriously handicapped when it tries to deal with transition.

Part FOUR

The Conclusion

Chapter Eight

A Practice Case

The mistakes are all there waiting to be made.
—S. A. TARTAKOWER, RUSSIAN CHESS MASTER, SPEAKING
OF THE CHESSBOARD AT THE BEGINNING OF A GAME

Six chapters ago you tried your hand at the case of the software company that wanted to form its individual contributors into service teams. Now I'll present another case to help you see if you can apply what you've been reading.

You work for Apex Manufacturing, a 4,000-employee firm that used to be the world's foremost company in its field: small, specialized gasoline motors. Together with two domestic competitors, which had been founded by alumni from your company, Apex made most of the world's supply of such motors—in 1980, Apex alone made 52% of the motors produced.

Since 1990, however, two Asian firms and one German company have entered the field, and one of Apex's American competitors has invested huge amounts of money in new plants and equipment. To make matters more difficult, new governmental noise abatement standards have forced Apex to re-design the motors' exhaust systems. Somehow, your competitors foresaw these new standards and built them into their new designs. You didn't, and so Apex has had to make costly modifications. By 2000, Apex had only 43% of the world's market, and that figure was falling.

There have been rumors for some time of impending plant consolidations and staff layoffs, but only a week ago the CEO was quoted in a *Wall Street Journal* article as saying that Apex would be able to do its trimming by attrition alone and that he expected sales figures to increase significantly by the end of the year. "We're just caught in one of those cycles," he said. "We'll have 50% of the world market again within two years."

Yesterday morning you received an e-mail message from the vice president of human resources asking you to come to a noontime meeting in her office.

When you got there, you saw a dozen of the company's most respected managers—everyone from supervisors to directors. The VP told you briefly that several decisions had just been made by the executive team.

First, two of the company's five plants will be closed, affecting 900 nonexempt workers and 100 exempts, about one-third of the company's manufacturing group. The situation will be complicated by several factors. The two plants made one of the company's more modern and successful lines of motors. The locations of the plants raised costs and led to their being pegged for closure. The plants must continue producing motors for at least eight more months while the other plants are readied to take up the slack in the production.

Second, there is to be a 20% reduction in the level of employment at the company—800 jobs. All departments are to make cuts, though specific targets for different groups have not yet been set. Neither have the provisions of a possible early retirement plan. It has not even been decided how many of the terminated employees will be from among the 1,000 extra manufacturing employees. Many of those people were long-term employees whom the VP of manufacturing wanted to reassign to one of the other plants or to some other part of the company.

"There are still a lot of questions," the human resources VP said. "But you are being called together as a transition management advisory group. The executive team made the decision as to *what* will be necessary—downsizing and consolidation. We're asking you to help us work out *how* we should do it. Specifically, you are being asked to come up with a scenario for announcing and implementing the closure and for working out a plan for handling the reductions in the workforce.

"We're going to meet together all day tomorrow," she continued, "and I want you to clear your calendars. We have to get a tentative plan back to the executive team by the end of the week. It doesn't have to be detailed, but it does have to sketch out the issues that we need to be ready to deal with and to give us some ideas for dealing with them. We want it to advise us on communications, training, and any new policies or arrangements we need to have in place to get people through the transition."

Then she handed out a sheet on which she had listed some of her own transition management concerns:

1. Apex has not had a layoff in the past twenty years. During most of that time it was growing.

2. The 1,000 workers from the two plants to be closed include some highly talented people whom the organization doesn't want to lose.

3. The leadership team strongly favors an across-the-board cut in employment levels ("It would be fairer"), but she and some others share a concern that some parts of the company are already dangerously lean while others are "fatter."

4. There is a perception among hourly employees that the senior managers, whose pay has always been generous, are not bearing enough of the brunt of the difficulties of the company they lead.

5. The basic announcement of the closure and downsizing decisions is scheduled to go out tomorrow in a memo to all employees. A copy is attached:

> To: All Apex Employees
> From: R. E. Owens, President and CEO
> Regarding: Measures Needed to Restore Profitability
>
> In order to recover ground lost to foreign competitors, who have been able to dump their government-subsidized products on the American market, the executive team has decided to consolidate all manufacturing into the plants at Worthington, San Jose, and Little Rock. The plants in Stevens Mills and Grandview will be phased out over the next eight or nine months.
>
> During the same period, employment levels in the company, which have recently risen past the 4,000 mark, will be readjusted to a level around 3,200. At that level we will be able to maintain profitability if we can contain other costs. In the latter regard, all employees are asked to refrain from ordering supplies and equipment unless it has been personally approved by a member of the senior management team.
>
> Apex has a noble tradition, but in recent years too many of our employees have forgotten that we must make a profit for our stockholders. If, however, we can tighten our belts and do more with less, we'll not only climb back into the black, but we'll also recover the market share that slipped through our fingers when we let ourselves get too comfortable.
>
> I will be back in touch with you when the details of the plant closures and the layoffs have been determined. In the meantime, I am sure that I can count on your continued hard work and loyalty.
>
> R. E. Owens
> President and CEO

"We're in a tight spot," the human resources VP concluded. "Frankly, I'm not sure all the senior managers realize how tight it is. I'm looking to you folks to help me make the case for handling the human side of this whole mess with some care. And I'm looking to you to help me show that there is, in fact, a way to do it that doesn't just drop everything on the people like a bomb and then leave them to take care of their own wounded.

"I'd suggest that you go back to your units and arrange to free up the next couple of days. Then I'd like you to look over the following list of suggestions that were made by different members of the senior management team and rate them on a scale of one to five.

"We'll compare reactions in the morning and come up with some first steps."

You go back to your office, ask the secretary to postpone and cancel your meetings, and start to work on the list of suggestions. (*Do that now. Write a number to the left of each item on the list. Finish doing so before you continue.*)

1 = Very important. Do this at once.

2 = Worth doing but takes more time. Start planning it.

3 = Yes and no. Depends on how it's done.

4 = Not very important. May even be a waste of effort.

5 = No! Don't do this.

_____ Cancel the memo and don't distribute any communications until firm plans have been made for the details of the layoffs and plant closures.

_____ Rewrite the memo to convey more sensitivity to the impact on the company's employees.

_____ Set up a "manufacturing restructuring task force" to recommend the best way to consolidate operations and determine the disposition of the 1,000 excess workers from the plants at Stevens Mills and Grandview.

_____ Set up a "downsizing suggestion plan" through which everyone can have input into how the downsizing will be carried out.

_____ Sell the problem that forced the changes.

_____ Fire the CEO. He's lost his credibility.

_____ Bring in all site managers and directors for an extensive briefing. Hold a no-holds-barred question-and-answer session. Don't let them leave until they're all satisfied that there is no better way to handle the situation.

_____ Make a video explaining the problem and the response to it. Hold all-hands meetings at each company site, with the site manager taking and answering all questions.

_____ Set up a hot line to give employees current, reliable information.

_____ Get the senior management team to agree to a one-year 20% cut in their own salaries.

_____ Order an across-the-board 20% budget cut throughout the company.

_____ Institute a program of rewards for cost-saving suggestions from employees.

_____ Plan closure ceremonies for the two plants.

_____ Use the time the company spends in the neutral zone to redesign the whole business: strategy, employment, policies, and structure.

_____ Get the CEO to make a public statement acknowledging the tardiness of the company's response to the realities of the marketplace.

_____ Make it clear up front that the company is headed into a protracted period of change.

_____ Explain the purpose of the announced changes, provide a picture and a plan for them, and describe the parts that people will be playing in them.

_____ Circulate an upbeat news release saying that this plan has been in the works for two years, that it isn't a sign of weakness, that its payoff will occur within a year, and so on. In all communications, accentuate the positive.

_____ Allay fears by assuring workers that the two plant closures are the only big changes that will take place.

_____ Develop or find career-planning seminars to help people whose jobs are being threatened or lost because of the changes.

_____ Immediately set new, higher production targets for the next quarter so that people will have something clear to shoot for and, by aiming high, adequate output will be ensured even if they fail to reach the goals.

_____ Make a video in which the CEO gives a fiery "we gotta get lean and mean" speech.

_____ Analyze who stands to lose what in the changes.

_____ Redo the compensation structure to reward compliance with the new system.

_____ Help the CEO put together a statement about organizational transition and what it does to an organization. The result should be empathetic and concerned about people.

_____ Set up Transition Monitoring Teams in the Stevens Mills and Grandview plants as well as in other units that are significantly affected by the changes.

_____ Appoint a "change manager" to be responsible for seeing that the changes go smoothly.

_____ Give everyone at Apex a "We're Number One!" badge.

_____ Put all managers through a quality improvement seminar.

_____ Reorganize the executive team and redefine the CEO's job as a "team coordinator."

_____ Give all managers a two-hour seminar on the emotional impacts of change.

_____ Plan some all-hands social events—picnics, outings, dinners—in each company location.

_____ Launch a plan to buy the smallest of Apex's domestic competitors to gain market share and a strong research and development group.

_____ Find ways to "normalize" the neutral zone and to redefine it in terms that have more benefit to both the organization and its employees.

As in chapter 2, the following comments are not meant to provide "right" answers but to raise issues so that you aren't overlooking the transition dimension of these changes.

Category 1: Very important. Do this at once.

Rewrite the memo to convey more sensitivity to the impact on the company's employees.   The current memo is a disaster. (Memos themselves are not the best way to convey information like this if an all-hands meeting is possible, though in a multi-site organization it isn't.) The tone of the memo disowns any leadership responsibility for the situation and leaves the impression that people haven't worked hard enough. See the following items for ways in which the public announcement could be improved, but at the head of the list needs to be "more sensitivity to the impact on the company's employees"!

Get the CEO to make a public statement acknowledging the tardiness of the company's response to the realities of the marketplace.   Whatever the CEO says, his credibility has already been compromised. Just a week ago he was telling a *Wall Street Journal* reporter that everything was going to be great. It's very important to address this credibility problem directly and quickly—and to take responsibility for past mistakes.

Make it clear up front that the company is headed into a protracted period of change.   This is the next step in the program of credibility-rebuilding. It is tempting to be "reassuring" and even to cut a few corners in an attempt to be. But that is very dangerous because the reassurance lasts only a little while, and what lasts a long time is the mistrust generated by false reassurances.

Sell the problem that forced the changes.   To do this, you'll first have to "sell the problem" of the transition-related problems to the CEO. Until he buys the problem, he isn't going to buy the solution, which is talking publicly about the organization's real problems. But until he's ready to do this, neither will he be able to sell any of his planned changes as the best way out of the company's difficult situation.

Help the CEO put together a statement about organizational transition and what it does to an organization. The result should be empathetic and concerned about people.   This depends, of course, on the CEO's *understanding* organizational transition. You may need to administer a little shock therapy to get the message across, and this will probably have to come from an outsider. In an organization that has hidden its head in the sand as long as this one has, it's hard for inner alarms to be heard. Assuming that you can get the CEO to understand the transition-related problems, his open discussion of them will set the tone for the whole transition management effort that is going to be necessary if the current changes are not to start the company sliding down the slope to disaster.

Bring in all site managers and directors for an extensive briefing. Hold a no-holds-barred question-and-answer session. Don't let them leave until they're all satisfied that there is no better way to handle the situation.   These men and women are going to have to answer a thousand questions from their people. They will have to feel the rightness of the actions in their bones. If they believe in what is being done, they will bring others along with them. If they don't, everyone is in trouble. Get this group on board immediately. Tell them the truth—even if some of it has to be withheld from others for the time being—and give them the chance to ask any and all questions. Don't pull punches with this group, and don't delay talking with them.

Make a video explaining the problem and the response to it. Hold all-hands meetings at each company site, where the site manager takes and answers all questions.   Perhaps this belongs in Category 2, because it obviously takes some time—although a simple video of the CEO (and perhaps others in the executive group) talking about the problems and their solutions to them could be put together pretty quickly. The video is part of the communications effort to get beyond memos and present at least the semblance of the leadership's personal communication. (It may work better for the leaders to make a rapid flying tour of the company's various locations.)

Appoint a "change manager" to be responsible for seeing that the changes go smoothly.   Even before the details of the changes are clear, it is certain that they will involve things that span different areas of authority and fall in no one's area of authority. Someone must oversee these things—the regular lines of authority aren't adequate. If the person appointed is someone with another position, some way must be found to relieve him or her from conflicting duties. The appointment could also go to someone who is taken out of his or her regular job completely and made the change manager for the duration of the changes. Realize, though, that this person acts as an overseer or a coordinator, not a boss.

Set up Transition Monitoring Teams in the Stevens Mills and Grandview plants, as well as in other units that are significantly affected by the changes. The leaders need new channels of upward communication—and need them immediately. The TMT is the easiest way to achieve this. Don't sit passively and listen. Engage the TMT in a dialogue, try ideas on them, ask for their advice, argue (nonbelligerently) with them—and then act on what they tell you. If you don't act, the TMT will quickly be tagged as just another management scam.

Category 2: Worth doing but takes more time. Start planning it.

Explain the purpose of the announced changes, provide a picture and a plan for them, and describe the parts that people will be playing in them. This is the heart of transition management, but it is impossible to do it right away. You can talk about the purpose (the *why* of the changes), but only the sketchiest kind of picture of the organization is going to come out of the changes. And the plan is only a plan for a couple of first steps. The Four P's are the planning group's agenda, but they are going to take months to work out in the detail necessary for their success. Besides, management first needs to concern itself with endings and neutral zone issues.

Analyze who stands to lose what in the changes. This is a critical task, but it is another one that takes time. It is not a onetime task, but rather an ongoing habit for people to develop as they plan and implement the thousands of changes that will be part of the big plan. (You might consider starting with what the CEO stands to lose by acknowledging that the response to the new market conditions has been dangerously tardy. Such losses may well stand in the way of his playing an effective leadership role, unless you can think of ways to help him let go.)

Give all managers a two-hour seminar on the emotional impacts of change. Determining who's going to lose what is just the first of many transition management tactics with which managers must become familiar. A short seminar, held as soon as possible, may be the best way to help people recognize that they have indeed lost something in these changes, that "grieving" is normal, and that it usually involves emotions like anger and depression, which are easily mistaken for "bad morale" and may even be punished.

Set up a hot line to give employees current, reliable information. You might put this in Category 1 because it is very important to provide fast, accurate, and reliable information. But don't set up a hot line until you've created reliable machinery to have it answered, to process the questions that it generates, and to return the answers to the questioners. Any communications medium that raises more questions than it answers is dangerous.

Set up a "manufacturing restructuring task force" to recommend the best way to consolidate operations and determine the disposition of the 1,000 excess workers from the plants at Stevens Mills and Grandview. What faces Apex is not simply a task of closing down a couple of plants or laying off 800 excess workers. The danger is that those changes, so formidable in themselves, will preoccupy people to the point that they forget that these changes were necessary because their organization had allowed itself to maintain a status quo that was daily growing more obsolete. If Apex is to be revitalized, its manufacturing must be redesigned. That is the megachange, and it needs to be designed by the people who have to make it work. Hence the task force, made up of a combination of the brightest critics within manufacturing and representatives of the group that now holds power. They will also need outside expertise, but no experts can do the job for them.

Develop or find career-planning seminars to help people whose jobs are being threatened or lost because of the changes. The 1,000 people displaced by the plant closures have just run into a solid wall in their career paths. They need help in rethinking their careers. So do the people displaced in the larger company reorganization that will surely take place. If you provide them with career assistance, those who leave the company will take with them a positive feeling about the organization because it helped them find work elsewhere, and those who stay will be grateful for the assistance in redirecting their efforts inside Apex. Lacking such help, the "leavers" will be angry and talk down the company at every chance, and the "stayers," bitter and frustrated, will undermine the company's ongoing operations.

Plan closure ceremonies for the two plants.   These places have been a home and a world to many people. They need a way to disengage themselves from that world. Some organizations hold funerals, some hold wakes, and some create unique ceremonies of closure. The details of what is done are far less important than the fact that representatives of the affected groups themselves do the planning and implementation. It has to be *their* event. The planning takes a great deal of time and is itself a therapeutic process. Start right away.

Institute a program of rewards for cost-saving suggestions from employees. What is happening at Apex is much more than simple cost-cutting, but saving money is an important part of the solution to the company's problems. Soliciting suggestions from employees is an important action. Not only does it draw on an often untapped expertise, but it also challenges people to be conscious of the costs of what they do. Employees will be engaged in the search for a solution rather than simply forced to accept solutions. (Consider giving them a slice of the savings; if they're sharing the pain, they ought to share the gain.)

Find ways to "normalize" the neutral zone and to redefine it in terms that benefit both the organization and its employees.   Take care of endings first, of course, but begin thinking about what is sure to be a long time in the wilderness. The journey from what Apex used to be to what Apex needs to become is going to last for several years. Like any confusing and ill-defined time, people are likely to project their fears onto it. You need to help them understand why they are so uncomfortable during this time. You must find a more meaningful metaphor for it. Remember the "sinking ship" versus the "ship's last voyage." The latter gave people a context in which they could help themselves and the organization. The former, which simply expressed everyone's fears, did not.

Use the time the company spends in the neutral zone to redesign the whole business: strategy, employment, policies, and structure.   This is the opportunity that is embedded in the dangerous situation in which Apex now finds itself. This is the chance—and in today's situation, probably the last chance Apex will get—to transform the company from yesterday's industry leader and today's critical case into tomorrow's comeback champion. Everyone's attention has been caught. The debates over the need to change have been decided. This is the time to seize the initiative and convert a necessary reorganization into a complete revitalization. This effort will take a long time, and it must be begun immediately. Only out of such a complete redesign effort can a convincing new picture of the organization emerge. Without such a picture, you're just pushing players around on the board with no strategy and no clear plan.

Category 3: Yes and no. Depends on how it's done.

Order an across-the-board 20% budget cut throughout the company. That's a huge cut, and if you simply order that it be made, the results are likely to be disastrous. A totally redesigned organization might well be able to turn out its present output or more for one-fifth less money. But you cannot take the old organization, lop off one-fifth of its resources, and tell it to keep on turning out the widgets at the old rate. Still, as a target figure, 20% is important. The divisions can use it as a guideline to generate savings of, say, 10%. The remaining 10% will probably have to come from discontinuing unproductive operations or having costly support services provided by outside vendors.

Get the executive team to agree to a one-year 20% cut in their own salaries. *This* has more merit. It is the kind of step that seizes people's imaginations and sends a clear message that the leadership is serious. The trouble is that if it is done by fiat, it generates hostility from the very people who have to lead the new charge on the opposition. So an executive pay cut can't be imposed. Senior managers must be made to understand the problem and the need for a powerful attention-getting symbolic action. They may need new evidence that what people believe to be their unfairly high pay is undermining their credibility. The problem is that there may be no one within the group who will champion this message. Everyone's immediate self-interest may get in the way of their long-term self-interest, which is to revitalize the company. This is one of the many areas in which outsiders may be useful.

Plan some all-hands social events—picnics, outings, dinners—in each company location.   In the neutral zone such events can help to protect or rebuild the solidarity that has been damaged by losses and the confusion people feel. But these events have to be timed effectively. Done at the wrong time, they take on a "bread and circuses" quality, like the giveaways and spectaculars that the late Roman emperors used to keep their restless subjects distracted and quiet. So deal with endings first, then consider such events.

Make a video in which the CEO gives a fiery "we gotta get lean and mean" speech.   Several things about this idea are wrong. First, the CEO hasn't yet done anything to restore his credibility—such as leveling with people or taking a 20% pay cut. Second, this isn't a time for organizational weight loss; instead, the whole organization needs to be redesigned. Third, "lean and mean" is a cliché that has lost much of its power to move people. To the extent that tightening and trimming are the answers, the need for them has to be communicated in a fresh and believable way.

Set up a "downsizing suggestion plan" through which everyone can have input into how the downsizing will be carried out.   We've already established that employee suggestions have many benefits and ought to be solicited—particularly on how to save money in the everyday conduct of business. There will also be a time for employee input into the redesign process. But to throw something as difficult and painful as layoffs open to "employee suggestions" is to court disaster. One way to involve employees in the process is to set up an employee group to advise management on selection criteria for deciding who should be terminated. The process may be no better than the one management would come up with itself, but involvement leads to buy-in. And management doesn't need any more processes that employees refuse to buy into.

Fire the CEO.   This has appeal. The guy sounds like a jerk. Maybe he lacks the wherewithal to get people through the next few years. But watch out. Companies often get the leadership they deserve, and to punish the leader for failures that were the product of many minds is just scapegoating. It's unfair, and it doesn't do any good. It may even strengthen the refusal of the CEO's loyal troops (and there may be many of them) to go along with whatever redesign effort is undertaken by a new leader. Beyond these considerations, a change in leadership at this time will bring a whole new army of changes into the field. Be sure that the gains exceed the costs. All this said, it is unlikely that this CEO will last more than a couple of years regardless of what you do. He is too tarred with the brush of failure to be able to lead a revitalized organization.

Category 4: Not very important.
May even be a waste of effort.

Launch a plan to buy the smallest of Apex's domestic competitors to gain market share and a strong research and development group.   At crisis points organizations sometimes turn outward to solve what are really internal problems. It's like the married couple who decide to have a new baby to save their marriage. The results are likely to be disastrous—not only because the solution doesn't solve anything, but also because the solution further burdens an already overburdened system. Yet the impulse to acquire what the company does not have is not all wrong. If it were part of the larger redesign, it might be a great move. But now it's not, so forget it.

Reorganize the executive team and redefine the CEO's job as a "team coordinator."   Again, the impulse may have some merit. Apex is an old-line company, and its governance system is probably outmoded. (Certainly it hasn't been making wise decisions lately.) *If* the redesign we have been discussing created a different kind of structure that demanded a different kind of governance, and *if* a more egalitarian culture emphasizing teamwork proved to characterize the new organization, then a leadership team run by a coordinator-CEO would make sense. But those are big "ifs." As an isolated change, it will more likely just deepen the mess everyone is in.

Put all managers through a quality improvement seminar.   Quality may indeed be an area in which Apex is losing ground to its competitors. But a quality improvement program is a major undertaking, one that generates a whole field of individual and group transitions. To overlay that on the reorganization that is now under way is asking for trouble. At a later point, when the picture is clearer, quality improvement may prove to be a critical piece of the outcome Apex is seeking. Until then, it's a 500-pound sack that you're going to load onto the back of an already overloaded camel.

Redo the compensation structure to reward compliance with the new system.   Maybe this too will prove to be a good idea somewhere down the line, after the Four P's are clearer. But for now, no new roles, attitudes, or behavior can be said unequivocally to deserve special reward. (The one exception is the bonus that should be paid for valuable suggestions.)

Category 5: No! Don't do this.

Cancel the memo and don't distribute any communications until firm plans have been made for the details of the layoffs and plant closures. This is guaranteed to turn confusion into total chaos. People know that something big is up. A pirated version of the CEO's unfortunate memo is likely to be faxing its way from site to site and office to office. The secretaries had the news before the VPs, so don't imagine that you can put a cap on this story. Instead, move forward with all the speed you can. Tell people what is afoot, and then tell them when they can expect to hear the next installment. If that deadline proves unworkable, tell them why and then tell them when they can expect the next communication. Don't let communications cease. People abhor a communications vacuum. Besides, the local business reporters are already at work on a story that will tell people more than you were planning to. So seize the communications initiative. Start talking.

Allay fears by assuring workers that the two plant closures are the only big changes that will take place. You can't say this! It's almost certain to be untrue. It will be perceived as one more of management's lies and another good reason "not to believe a damned thing they say." It's far better to say that these are the only changes that have been decided on at present but that further changes will undoubtedly have to be made and that people will learn of them as soon as they have been decided on.

Immediately set new, higher production targets for the next quarter so that people have something clear to shoot for and, by aiming high, adequate output will be ensured even if they fail to reach the goals. These tactics are getting worse and worse. It's almost certain that output is going to fall, at least temporarily. When that happens, people who already feel inadequate will have evidence that their feelings are right. Far better to set lower targets and exceed them than to achieve slightly higher productivity and a lasting sense of failure.

Circulate an upbeat news release saying that this plan has been in the works for two years, that it isn't a sign of weakness, that its payoff will occur within a year, and so on. In all communications, accentuate the positive. "Be positive!" is one of those dangerous half-truths that are constantly snagging us on the false half. It's important for people to be led by others who believe and say,

"We can make it," but it's very dangerous to leave the impression that the path will be easy or that the outcome is certain. Far too much positiveness consists in leaving that impression. Realism is increasingly important as people get further into the redesign process. By that time they can see what they're up against. And "positive thinking" is likely to sound more and more like "wishful thinking."

Give everyone at Apex a "We're Number One!" badge.   Apex can barely stay afloat! Somebody has been watching too many basketball playoff games. This is the worst kind of positive thinking—not to mention being irrelevant. Not a good combination. Mottos are useful, but only when they effectively capture a real emerging possibility. When they are just words, they simply reinforce what is probably already too prevalent an opinion: this company is being led by a bunch of jerks!

Well, how did you do? Better than in chapter 2, I bet. In categorizing these options, I found myself debating which rating to give several of them, and if I did it again I might do it differently. The idea is not to put all the items in the same categories that I did, but to make decisions *with people in mind.*

Whatever plans the leadership at Apex (or you yourself) come up with are going to represent changes in the world that people have known. Such changes create transitions, and transitions have to take place if the changes are to work. The odds of transitions actually taking place as planned will rise greatly if you make your decisions with the basic transition management tactics in mind.

Chapter Nine

Conclusion

A great war leaves a country with three armies: an army of cripples, an army of mourners, and an army of thieves.
—GERMAN PROVERB

This proverb comes from centuries of experience with the traumatic changes that accompany conquest, and it deserves at least a footnote in any organizational plan for strategic change. It reminds us that whatever positive results the conquerors gain by their efforts, they leave behind three serious problems: the survivors who have been wounded by the changes they have been through; those who are grieving over all that they have lost in the change; and those whose loyalty and ethics have been so compromised by their experience that they turn hostile, self-centered, and subversive. To make matters worse, in the struggles surrounding organizational change, these "three armies" are found on the winning side as well as on the losing side.

The problem of survivors is seldom on the minds of the planners of change, but it cannot be avoided by anyone who must implement the change or by the people who must manage the situation that results from it. In the aftermath of the Manville Corporation's asbestos-driven bankruptcy, *Boardroom Reports* interviewed S. R. Heath, the company's executive vice president for administration. He talked mainly about the problem of survivors. Manville's liabilities had forced a Chapter 11 bankruptcy filing and a workforce reduction of almost 40%. Heath was asked what surprised him the most about this painful process. "I guess it was the problems of the survivors," he replied. "We didn't realize that the survivors would need as much help as those who were leaving. We were focusing most of our efforts on those departing. . . . We ultimately determined that professional help was needed to rebuild the teams and relationships that were disturbed by the layoffs."

Not all organizations have to face the prospect of such deep cuts, but Heath's comments must be taken seriously by the leaders of any organization that is considering a reorganization or a personnel cutback of significant scope. One of the ironies of today's organizational world is that the current mania for trimming the organizational waistline is justified in the name of organizational health. Having made these cuts, organizations discover that the only sustainable source of cost savings is a greater and more efficient effort by their employees. Unfortunately, those employees are the same "survivors" referred to in the German proverb—employees whose energy has been sapped and whose commitment has been weakened by unmanaged or mismanaged transition.

> *The leavers have adjusted better than the stayers.*
>
> EXXON VICE PRESIDENT, DESCRIBING THE AFTERMATH OF THE COMPANY'S DOWNSIZING

One of the ironies of the organizational world is that outplacement services have become an accepted way to assist terminated employees but no comparable body of services has been developed to help those who are left behind. There are really two ironies there. The first is that money and effort are being devoted to people who can no longer contribute to the success of the company. The survivors, on whose efforts and motivation the future of the company depends, get little or no attention. The second irony is that the kinds of training that are given to terminated employees by an outplacement program are designed to equip them to find work and manage their careers in a continually changing business environment. This is the kind of training that all employees need in a rapidly changing environment, but these newly trained former employees are now working for the company's competitors.

I think of such matters whenever I read articles about the changes that today's organizations are being urged to make to become competitive or profitable. *INC.* magazine ran such an article, listing "Ten Commandments" that present-day manufacturing companies need to abide by to be successful:

1. Keep production units small.

2. Keep corporate overhead low.

3. Keep productivity high.

4. Keep production flexible.

5. Remain market driven.

6. Customize products.

7. Strive for margins, not volume.

8. Stress customer service.

9. Recruit from the New America [i.e., outside the white, male, young mainstream].

10. Recruit a CEO with nonmanufacturing experience.[1]

All of these things make good sense, but think of the transitions that any of them—much less all ten at once—would cause an existing company to go through if they were introduced. Each of these changes would force people to let go of their old worlds, leave them in the neutral zone for an extended period, and then call on them to learn new behaviors and develop new attitudes. The *INC.* list and others like it are recommending transition times ten.

Today's organizations are reeling from the human impacts of the changes that have been forced on them by new technology, international competition, new regulations, and changing demographics. What is the prescription for this condition? More change. It is like taking a big drink ("the hair of the dog that bit you") as a hangover remedy. It is actually worse than that, for when the change does not cure this hangover, the organization tries another change—and then another—in rapid succession.

We are still caught in the mid-twentieth-century mindset, which conceived of the main organizational problem as *the lack of change.* That outlook led to the idea of the "change agent"—a person who knew how to enter an organization, often from outside, and change things. But as we enter the twenty-first century, we're increasingly faced with the fact that *the current problem is change itself.* It's the problem of "survivors" of yesterday's change projects, and everyone is a survivor.

This is why transition management is such a critical skill for you to develop. You're going to find yourself dealing with the aftermath of mismanaged or unmanaged transition every time you turn around. That aftermath is a manager's nightmare. To remind myself of its characteristics, I use the acronym GRASS:

Guilt: Managers (including you) feel guilty that they have had to terminate, transfer, and demote people. Workers who survived when others were cut feel guilty too. Guilt lowers self-esteem and often leads to one of two kinds of overcompensation: permissiveness to make up for the earlier harsh acts, or an even harsher "blaming the victim," which projects the responsibility for the guilt away from the person who feels it.

Resentment: Everyone, manager and managed alike, feels angry at the organization for the pain that transition causes. This is natural. But when that

The winners of tomorrow will deal proactively with chaos, will look at the chaos per se as the source of market advantage, not as a problem to be got around.

Tom Peters,
American writer

aspect of the grieving process is not managed sensitively, the anger deepens and lengthens into a continuing resentment that poisons the whole organization. When yesterday's changes leave such a legacy of resentment, today's changes are undermined even before they are launched. In addition, resentment leads to sabotage and the subtler forms of pay-back that organizations experience today.

Anxiety: People who are trying to hold on to the past while pieces of it are being cut away are anxious. The strange thing is that some managers believe that anxiety improves motivation. Perhaps a little bit of anxiety does that, but in the quantity that is common in organizations today, anxiety reduces energy, lowers motivation, and makes people unwilling to take the risk of trying new things.

Self-absorption: Anxious people become preoccupied with their own situations and lose their concern for fellow workers or customers. In a game of musical chairs, the only real questions are, "When is the music going to stop?" and "Will there be a chair left for me?" Larger issues of teamwork, good service, and high quality get fuzzy when the focus is so nearsightedly personal as this. Nor do pep talks on the values of teamwork, good service, and high quality do much good when people are self-absorbed. People simply do not absorb inspiration well in that state.

Stress: I've already talked about the increase in the rate of illness and accident when people are in transition. Most organizations respond with stress management programs. These programs are certainly better than nothing, but they do little to counter the sources of stress. Creating stress and then trying to "manage" it is like trying to cool your overheated brakes. The only real answer is to stop overheating them.

GRASS: Guilt, Resentment, Anxiety, Self-absorption, and Stress. These are the five real and measurable costs of not managing transition effectively. Remember them the next time people tell you there isn't time to worry about the reactions of your employees to the latest plan for change. And help such people to see that not managing transition is really a shortcut that costs much more than it saves. For it leaves behind an exhausted and demoralized workforce at the very time when everyone agrees that the only way to be successful is to get more effort and more creativity out of the organization's employees.

How poor are they that have not patience! What wound did ever heal but by degrees?

WILLIAM SHAKESPEARE,
BRITISH DRAMATIST

The other thing to remember and help others to understand is that there are well-tested, effective ways to avoid these difficulties. Many organizations follow the path toward their own collapse simply because they do not know that there is another way.

This is all the more important today, because if we know anything about the future, it is that it will be different from the present. *Whatever currently exists is going to change.* What it will look like is something that the futurists can debate. The only certainty is that between *here* and *there* will be a lot of change. Where there's change, there's transition. That's the utterly predictable equation:

$$change + human\ beings = transition$$

There's no way to avoid it. But you can manage it. And if you want to come through in one piece, you *must* manage it.

> *Our moral responsibility is not to stop the future, but to shape it . . . to channel our destiny in humane directions and to ease the trauma of transition.*
>
> ALVIN TOFFLER,
> AMERICAN FUTURIST

---

1. "Ten Commandments of Manufacturing," *INC.* (November 1990), p. 21.

Assessing Your Transition Readiness

Whenever I start a project with an organization, I do an informal evaluation of how ready the organization is for the transition it faces. Some organizations seem to function in such a way that transition is taken in stride, while others—which may be just as successful as the first group in most other ways—find that transition disrupts their operations and distresses their people so much that the particular change that put them into the transition is hardly worth the trouble it causes. In some cases, a change that was supposed to strengthen an organization ends up weakening it.

Here's what I look for when I talk with people while setting up the project and as I interview them in the course of my consulting, coaching, or training. These are the questions I ask explicitly, or look for answers to, as I talk with people, read the survey data they have gathered, and review the communications that have been sent out by the leaders.

1. Is there a fairly widespread sense that the change is necessary? Is the change solving a real problem, or do people think that it is happening for some other reason? Nothing is harder to stomach than losses and uncertainty that you believe "didn't have to happen."

2. Do most people accept that whatever change is taking place represents a valid and effective response to the underlying problem? A "bad idea" is going to produce a transition that is particularly hard to manage.

3. Has the proposed change polarized the workforce in any way that is going to make the transition more disruptive than it would otherwise have been?

4. Is the level of trust in the organization's leadership adequate? There are always minor issues on this score, but when the level of trust is low, the leaders have a very hard time bringing the people along with them.

5. Does the organization provide people with adequate training for the new situations and roles that it thrusts them into? An organization that doesn't do that is likely to find people holding back and resisting the new beginning that will make the transition work as intended.

6. Does the organization tend to blame people if they make mistakes in a new situation? If it does, people are going to wait for others to make the first move as they start to emerge from the neutral zone, and the organization will stay in transition longer than it needs to.

7. Is the change part of a widely understood strategy that is designed to move the organization in a direction that fits with a fairly clear vision of the future?

8. Have the endings that are implicit in this change been talked about publicly? Do people know what it is time to let go of—and why?

9. Does the organization's history work in its favor during times of transition, or are there old scars and unresolved issues that surface and make people uncertain and mistrustful?

10. Has the change been explained to those who are going to be affected by it in as much detail as is currently possible?

11. Are there people within the organization who have expertise in the handling of change and transition? Is their assistance available to others in the organization who may need it?

12. Has a clear set of responsibilities been established for seeing that the human side of the change goes well? Do the people with those responsibilities have the resources to get their task done?

13. Do the leaders of the change understand that the *transitions* will necessarily take considerably longer to complete than the *changes?* Does the timetable for the project reflect that understanding?

14. Has the organization set up some way to monitor the state of the transition? This would not necessarily be a Transition Monitoring Team, but something more than the everyday reporting relationships in the organization.

15. Does the culture of the organization validate the idea of helping employees deal with the problems they encounter, or are they pretty much on their own?

These fifteen questions, either asked directly or used as an unspoken framework for conversations, will give you a pretty good idea of whether your organization will move through transition without undue difficulty, or whether the change is going to cause the organizational equivalent of a train wreck. The more negative answers these questions generate, the more difficulty lies ahead. While it is very hard to quantify the results, I'd be worried about an organization that generated fewer than ten yeses.

Needless to say, you have to talk to a real cross-section of the organization's people to answer the questions adequately. The leaders may be so out of touch with the situations that the average employee faces that they will give you very distorted answers. If the HR group is your sole source of information, you may get answers that are slanted by their sources of information and their agenda. The middle managers, the supervisors, the sales staff, the international division, the hourly workers—all of them have their own particular perspective, which will trap you if it is the only one you have. The way to avoid being trapped, of course, is to get your information from as wide a set of sources as possible.

Planning for Transition

You wouldn't launch a big change without a plan, and although you cannot make a *transition* happen according to plan as precisely as you can make a *change* happen, there are nonetheless some actions you ought to take to make sure it goes as well as it can. Here they are:

1. Share the problem—the one that makes the change necessary (or at least wise) before you try to share the change itself. And don't wait until the change is just about to happen.

2. Collect *information* about the problem from those closest to it; find out the *interests* that people are going to try to protect when they are exposed to the change; engage people in the problem-solving process to gain their *investment* in its outcome; and work to secure the *influence* of the most effective opinion makers. Information, interests, investment, and influence are the "Four I's" of transition planning.

3. At the same time—which is usually before the change is publicly announced—do an audit of the organization's transition-readiness (see appendix A) to discover the strengths and weaknesses that the organization brings to the experience of transition.

4. Educate the leaders about the nature of transition and how it differs from change. Make sure that they understand that an unmanaged transition can very easily make the change unmanageable. Help them to recognize that transition can in fact be managed and that leaders have a special role in making it manageable (see appendix E). Otherwise, they will be focused only on seeing that the change happens and they won't do what they need to do to bring the people along with them.

5. Get everyone who is planning the change to give serious thought to the question, "*Who* is going to have to let go of *what* to make the change work as planned?" Changes require transitions, and transitions require people to let go of how things used to be. Foreseeing and planning how to encourage that process is very important—and the part of transition management that organizations most often forget.

6. Recognize that people will not (because they *cannot*) move straight from letting go to making the new beginning. In between is the neutral zone, and that is a kind of organizational vacuum in which many things don't work well. Turnover often rises during that time; some employees become very angry and look for ways to "pay the organization back" for what it has done to them; productivity is likely to sag; and communication often breaks down. This is a time for hands-on leadership and the kind of management that people need in uncertain and ambiguous times.

7. The neutral zone is also a time when individuals and organizational units ought to step back and take stock. Find ways to encourage that. Such stock-taking enables people to move forward toward a *new* future—the one created by the changes—and to modify their strategy and resources in order to do so. It is in the neutral zone that individuals and groups reorient themselves from the old way to the new way. If they do not have the time or resources to do that, the new way simply won't work.

8. Monitor the progress of individuals and groups through the three stages of transition—using a Transition Monitoring Team or some other formal method of doing so (see appendix C). Pay as much attention to bottom-up communication as you do to top-down, and work to close the gap between decisionmakers (who may be nearly finished with their transitions) and ordinary employees (who may still be struggling with endings). Encourage groups to move forward through the transition, but do not let difficulty with the transition become a mark of shame.

9. Plan how you are going to explain, encourage, and reward the new behavior and attitudes that the changes are going to require of people. It is fine to talk about "the vision" and "the big picture," but remember that most people live at a much more practical level that is full of details. That is the level at which they are going to either contribute to the change or get in the way of it. Help them to understand what they can do to contribute to the change at that level.

10. All along the way, keep track of what helps and what hinders the organization and its people as they go through transition. At one level, this will help you to modify anything about the organization that makes transition harder to manage. At another level, it will provide you with some useful information about what works and what doesn't when you are trying to help people through the three stages of transition. Given the frequency of change today, such learning is guaranteed to come in very useful—and probably sooner than you imagine that it will.

Setting up a Transition Monitoring Team

No matter how carefully you prepare for a transition, you are going to be handicapped by the fact that there is no way to foresee all of the effects of the change or all of the reactions to it. That's why a Transition Monitoring Team (TMT) is so useful. The size of the team should be no more than a dozen or so and it may be better to set up several teams for different parts of the organization than to put too many people on one team (or stretch members too thin).

There are several ways to set up a team, each with its advantages and disadvantages. Where there are many groups to be represented, it may be most useful to *appoint* people to the team so that you get the best possible coverage of levels, ethnic groupings, shifts, old- and new-timers, and so on. The drawback, of course, is that the handpicked team may be seen as management stooges. So the selections need to include a few people who are clearly not management favorites—perhaps one or two who are known to be management critics. (This has the side effect of educating those people about the realities of the change.)

Where the pool of workers is not very large and it is more important to get people who are interested in the project than it is to get a carefully crafted cross-section, you can explain the task and ask for volunteers. You can also combine the two methods by having management choose from a pool of volunteers or by having different groups nominate candidates for the team, with management making final selections.

However the team is chosen, it has to be educated. Part of the education is about transition, because this is not a general feedback channel but a way to find out the effects that transition is having on people. Are any groups getting forgotten in the rush toward the future? Is the communication getting through—and is it being believed? Are any groups having particular trouble letting go of the old way of doing things? Are there any policies, practices, or structures that are impeding transition? What information, skills, or assistance do people need?

The team must also be educated about its area of responsibility, which is to operate as a *monitoring* team, not a *management* team. They may otherwise believe that they have been selected to lead the change project. The group should remain clear that its purpose is feedback.

The team should meet as long as there are transition issues to keep track of, although if that time extends beyond a year or so, it is probably a good idea to phase in new people gradually to replace the original members. (Phasing in new people also has the advantage of getting more people involved in and knowledgeable about the monitoring process.) The team must meet regularly and frequently enough to be able to deal with issues while they are still fresh. Many teams find that meeting every two weeks is about right, but sometimes events call for more frequent meetings. As the change winds down, the meetings can be held less frequently.

The meetings themselves need to be scheduled and run by a facilitator, and it is often useful to make that person a nonparticipant. Perhaps an HR person can take on the responsibility of sending out e-mails to remind people of upcoming meetings, running the meetings, and carrying the results of the meetings back to decisionmakers. It is advantageous if the facilitator happens to occupy an organizational role that gives her or him ready access to decisionmakers, because the output of the meetings is information that these people ought to know.

Initially, people may be suspicious of TMT members, wondering if they are management spies. That suspicion is itself a sign (though not an uncommon one) of mistrust within the organization, and mistrust is a situation that the decisionmakers need to address before it damages their undertaking. Often the mistrust dies out as soon as people start to discover that their worries and difficulties are being recognized by the TMT— and better yet, that they are being answered and remedied as a result of being brought up in TMT meetings. Some TMTs function very well by taking a passive role, simply reporting what people come to them and say, while other TMTs take a more active role, sending members around to interview people as part of their ear-to-the-ground effort.

It is generally wise to limit the focus of the TMT discussions to matters that have grown directly out of the changes going on in the organization and the transitions that people are in because of them. Inevitably, the group finds itself touching on more general matters ("how bad communication is around here," for example), and it is a good idea to find some way to channel those issues into appropriate venues for discussion and response. It is the facilitator's role to take care of this, but if some members of the TMT are also part of other groups that address organizational problems, these issues can be passed off to them on the spot.

It is often important to feed back information on specific issues to the groups and individuals who originally brought them to the TMT's attention. People naturally wonder what ever happened to their question or complaint or idea, and nothing kills a feedback system faster than people experiencing it as a black hole into which things are drawn and then disappear.

TMTs are extremely worthwhile, for they identify at an early stage problems that could later have serious consequences. They are one of the ways in which people can feel that they have a role (and a stake) in a change that has been planned by upper-level executives without much input from the rank and file. TMTs are also an effective way to counter rumors, because members of the team may be able to disseminate accurate information more believably than leaders can.

Appendix D

Career Advice for Employees of Organizations in Transition

If an organization is exposed to so much change that transition becomes a more or less continuous state, certain things happen to opportunities for employment and advancement. To put it simply, a lot of the opportunities go away. Cutting out a layer of management may have improved communications, for example, but it also removed a lot of positions that people had their eye on. Many organizations lose a whole "generation" of opportunities. That is when people start to grumble bitterly that "this place used to be a good place to work, but now there's no opportunity here anymore."

It is true that change destroys old opportunities, but it is equally true that it creates new ones. The same "flattening" of the organization that sliced out the layer of management jobs that people were after may also have created a number of self-managed groups. That self-management has created a role for a new kind of person: someone who can handle the external interfaces between the team and other parts of the organization. Another example: a reorganization that decentralizes your department and destroys your future job may also create a need for people who can manage virtual (nonlocalized) "teams" and work with groups dispersed over several locations. So what change does is not to destroy opportunities but to reconfigure the opportunity structure within an organization.

Obviously, a person who is trying to live with change would do well to find ways to capitalize on it. (Too many people simply try to figure out how to keep change from affecting them.) You need to go beyond "adjusting to change." In a time of constant change, getting adjusted to a change is no better than getting adjusted to the status quo, because the change *is* the new status quo. So how do you take advantage of frequent change?

The first thing you need to do is to stop thinking in terms of fixed "jobs" and start thinking in terms of the "unmet needs" or the "things that need doing" or the "unsolved problems" in the organization. It may help to think of the organization—or of the part of it you know best—as a *market* or a collection of (potential) customers who are seeking to get their needs met. Since they are probably as job-minded as you used to be, they keep wondering whose job it is to do what they need done.

If you don't act but simply let the situation take its own course, you may find quite a few new consultants and contract workers cruising the hallways, because today it is very common for organizations to enlist the aid of so-called free agents to get their needs met. But organizations do not need to do that, and yours will be less likely to if you act. *You* could play that free agent role for them—or you could if you wanted to. How would you set yourself up to do that? I'd suggest that you take what I call the Five JobShift Steps[1]:

Step 1: You start by finding out what resources you bring to anyone who needs some help. I urge you to think of those resources as being made up of four parts:

1. What you really want—because your Desires lead to powerful motivation. Wanting something a lot makes you work hard, and hard work is something that people need today.
2. Consider your Abilities. What are you good at?
3. What is your Temperament? What kind of activity are you naturally most suited to?
4. What are your Assets? What special knowledge or skill or experience, what contacts or qualifications (a certificate, a degree?), do you happen to have?

Together, Desires, Abilities, Temperament, and Assets represent the DATA that you bring to the table. They are your resources.

Step 2: Then you have to survey and understand the "market" you are trying to serve: Who are these customers? What are they after? What are the problems these customers are trying to solve? What are the specifications for the desired products or services? You are going to have to learn something about the customers you are proposing to serve. It'll take a little work, but all the better! That way you won't have so many people competing with you.

Step 3: Next, you combine your DATA and the unmet needs you find in the market. This combination—call it "what-I-have-that-you-need"—is your "product." Your product is a solution to a particular customer problem, a way of getting a result that the customer can't presently get but that he or she wants to get. You are no longer an employee doing a job. You are more like an independent worker (who just happens to be an "employee" too) who is selling a product. Many times you'll find that the customer would be willing to pay more for your product than the company was paying you as a wage. Good deal! If you keep finding that to be true, you may have to reconsider your employee status.

Step 4: If you start to see yourself as "selling a product" rather than "doing a job," you are in business for yourself, no matter whether you work inside the company or outside it. What business are you in—not your company's business but *yours?* You don't know? Well, don't feel too bad. Most of your fellow workers don't know either, so when you figure out the answer you'll have a head start on them.

Step 5: If you are in business, you are a micro-company—even if you are technically an employee. Stop thinking about your career. Start thinking about your business's *strategic plan.* Where is "You & Co." headed? What resources does it need? How can it market its services, whether inside your employer or outside?

The Five JobShift Steps will shift your mindset from that of an employee who *does a job* to that of an independent worker who *provides a customer with what he or she needs.* You say that this doesn't fit your needs because you want to remain an employee? Fine. What do companies need today? Workers who will deliver the best possible service or product to their customer—that's what. And this is the way to deliver the best.

When you start to approach work this way, you may find yourself fighting managers who aren't as far-sighted as you are. They may even tell you to wise up and just "do your job." You can find another place to work, where results are more important and managers are a little less conventional in their thinking. But if you're not in too big a hurry, hang in there, and you'll find that the world is coming around your way.

I'd say that the best advice for developing a career in an age of constant change is to stop doing a job and start finding the work that needs doing, the work that draws on your DATA and produces a "product" that somebody really needs. That is what I did more than twenty years ago when I decided that the unmet need of people around me was a way to deal successfully and productively with the high levels of change. I decided that my DATA fitted the task of speaking and writing on this subject. And that is what I have done ever since. This book is one of my products. I hope that you find it useful.

---

1. This is a very brief overview of the Five JobShift Steps, which I describe in much more detail in my book *Creating You & Co.: How to Think Like the CEO of Your Career* (Cambridge: Perseus Publishing, 1997).

The Leader's Role in Times of Transition

Everyone knows that one of the leader's most important roles is to "lead change," but too few people realize that that job goes nowhere unless the leader can also play a *transition* leadership role. These two roles overlap, but there is a basic difference between them. In relation to the change, the leader's task is to determine (usually in collaboration with others) the outcome of the change project and to keep reminding people what that outcome is and why it is important to achieve it.

The leader's transition task, on the other hand, is to lead people through it. Moses is a good model of transition leadership: he persuaded the Israelites to leave the status quo behind in Egypt, guided them through the wilderness, and, as the leadership mantel passed to Joshua, led them into a new beginning with a new identity.[1] The transition leader's task is to do a number of things related to getting people through the three phases of transition. Since there is a period before those three phases and one after they are concluded, it might be more accurate to say that the leader needs to think of his transition function as a play with five acts:

Act 1: Before the Transition

The transition hasn't started yet, but you know that a change is in the works. Others—including some of the executive team—may not know this yet, but that does not mean that the task of transition leadership hasn't started. This is the time to start "selling the problem" if you haven't done so already. Some leaders resist doing this because they are afraid that it will upset their followers. But then they are angry at those followers for not moving forward more quickly when the announcement is made. The people must acknowledge that there is a problem and understand the cost of not addressing it before they can follow the leader into action.

This leadership role may put you into your own transition, because it may force you to let go of your old way of leading, which may have been to keep quiet about problems whenever possible. That style of leadership, with its insistence on staying positive and upbeat, is one of the reasons why today's leaders and their organizations have so much trouble with transition.

The second thing that you need to do at this preliminary stage of managing the transition is to put together a one-minute speech about what the change is and why it is necessary. It won't be possible at this early date to give the details of the change, but it should be possible to give a rough sense of when additional information will be available. You'll use this one-minute speech again and again to deliver the basic message in a way that ensures consistency.

The final thing that can be done in advance is to assess employees' level of trust in the organization's leaders. Low trust means trouble in times of transition, so anything that can be done to build trust is worth doing. This is a time to be particularly careful to say what you'll do and then to do what you say. It is a time to strengthen emotional bonds between leaders and followers and to build a stronger sense that everyone is in the same boat. Needless to say, words count for little whenever it becomes evident that people are actually in a very different boat from their more privileged leaders. Remember: your actions and the situations that they create are sending messages that far outweigh your words.

Act 2: During the Ending

You need to be careful at this point not to overreact to resistance and opposition. Remember that what people are resisting is not the change that you spent so much energy on and that is so essential to the organization's future. What they are resisting is having to let go of things that they have always done or situations that they have depended upon for years. Understand that people are having to dismantle both their individual and collective worlds—those circumstances and outlooks that have helped them to feel at home at work. Cut people a little slack while they mourn their losses. Don't take aspects of that mourning, like anger or depression, out of context and turn them into personal challenges to your authority.

Remember that during endings people crave information, although, ironically, they sometimes have trouble remembering it after you have given it to them. If people seem distracted, remember that mourning involves a very complicated inner sorting process by which they let go of things that are going away and shift their attention to things that are staying. That takes a surprising amount of energy.

Leaders play an important part in this process by being the ones who define what it is time to let go of and what people do not have to let go of. Some leaders shy away from that task, fearing that focusing on endings will depress people. But remember: it is the fact of an ending, not naming it, that depresses people. A leader who shies away from saying what it is time to let go of is a leader who later finds that people haven't let go of the past and are stuck in the middle of transition long after they should have made a new beginning.

Leaders need to realize that they communicate more by actions than by words, but during a time of transition leaders may be relying too much on words. This often leads to mixed opportunities to send a clear message through timely and symbolic actions. Visiting a distant site, providing timely assistance, allocating space or money in a new way, reassigning a leader who has been ambivalent about a change, putting on a ceremonial or celebratory event to mark the turning point in a process—any of these actions can help to dramatize an ending and send the message that it is time to let go of the old way of doing things.

Act 3: In the Neutral Zone

In the neutral zone people feel lost and confused. What are the rules? Who's in charge of what? What does the new strategy do to the old priorities? They've had to let go of some things that all human beings need, and they need help finding replacements. It will help you understand the issues here to remember the acronym CUSP: people need (but currently lack) Control, Understanding, Support, and a clear sense of Priorities. As you watch your people struggle to adjust to the changes, remember that they are searching for ways to . . . :

> . . . *get more control of their situations:* Anything you can do to help people feel more in control of their work, their futures, and their lives in general is helpful.

> . . . *understand what is happening to them:* People function better when they understand the organization's actions and when they understand the transition process itself. Using transition terms ("ending," "neutral zone," "beginning") helps people to see why they are feeling what they are feeling.

> . . . *recover the feeling of being supported:* Most people had some kind of a support system before the change came along, but change disrupts support systems. During this difficult time, you can offer emotional support, which requires empathy or the ability to imagine the world from another's viewpoint, and you can also make sure that the organization is providing people with the practical support they need.

Clarify the new priorities and reinforce them in practice with examples and rewards.

This is the time when it is particularly important for you to express whatever concern you feel for employees and managers. (I put it that way because leaders who really don't care about their followers usually send that message so clearly through their behavior that any words they say to the contrary only mark them as hypocrites.) One action that clearly expresses concern is listening; good communication during the neutral zone has less to do with what you say than with your ability to really hear what others are saying. The TMT is one way to hear, and informal meetings with employees is another.

The neutral zone is also a time to step back and take stock of your own situation. Nothing undermines your ability to lead so much as difficulty handling your own transition. No one leads an organization through a transition without discovering that the leader's own role is changed in the process. Changes in organizational strategy, priorities, cultural values, or business processes may call into question personal plans that you had earlier taken for granted. These changes may also open up new opportunities, although that in turn may require that you make a change—and, of course, a transition. In such cases, you need to ask what it is time to let go of and then follow the path of transition yourself.

Act 4: During the New Beginning

It is important that leaders not be so in love with the details of the changes they are launching that they sacrifice the spirit of the outcome that the changes were intended to produce. Leaders who become emotionally wedded to their "plans" sometimes fail to distinguish between incidentals and fundamentals and end up establishing the former at the expense of the latter. This shows up when a TMT reports that some particular plan isn't working as it was intended to and, instead of responding flexibly, the leader insists on following the letter of a law that is unworkable. Beginnings go better when there is enough flex in the system that people can customize situations to fit them. Leaders who understand that can bring people out into whatever Promised Land they've been heading for. Leaders who don't understand that spend so much time looking for the *intended* entrance into the Promised Land that they never get in.

Good transition leaders automatically think of rewarding new behavior and attitudes, while those who are not very good at getting people through transition sometimes view praise and other forms of reinforcement as something that should not be necessary in view of how important the change is. You need to remember that when people are trying out new behaviors that don't yet feel normal or natural, rewards can be disproportionately effective.

You also need to remember that you are much further into the new beginning than your followers are. You have known about the change for much longer, you have a bigger-picture view of the reasons for it, you may be more familiar with alternatives to the old way of doing things than others are, and your identity may well be less tied to the old way of doing things than other people's are. It is also important not to take your advantages personally—that is, it is unlikely that you are further along in your transition than others because you are smarter or a better person. You are simply going to be able to make your new beginnings before your followers are, and until the followers catch up, they are going to have different needs than you do. You must realize that not everyone has the same outlook or needs as you do.

Act 5: After the Transition

Most leaders just bounce from one change to the next, but every change represents a chance to take stock of how you and the organization actually fared during the transition that the change generated. Such stock-taking (and the improvements in style and method and resources that can come from it) is a critical element of organizational improvement efforts and needs to be part of any significant change. Few organizations are set up—in either their form or their functions—to make times of transition go more smoothly, but such times are almost constant today. And most organizations run as though they were not. (Most executives, not coincidentally, also function as though transition were an occasional state of affairs rather than the way things are today.)

But enhancing an organization's transition-ability, or that of its leaders, is one of those ideas that gets back-burnered unless some senior leader gets behind them. Part of leading an organization through transition is assessing and enhancing its ability to deal with transition. Unfortunately, the pace of change these days is such that many leaders are in too big a hurry to do this. They are like an organization I consulted with in the mid-1980s: this business was so concerned with opening new manufacturing facilities and closing old ones that it never developed a standard way to do either. Every time, the process had to be invented from scratch—at least until somebody said, "Hey, we've done this before. We must know how to do it." Actually, it was one of their *leaders* who said it.

---

1. That Moses did not enter the Promised Land symbolizes the fact that the style of leadership has to change as a new beginning is being launched. The transformation of the people is finished at that point, and a more "transactional" sort of leader is needed. That was Joshua, a much more conventional figure than Moses. In modern organizational settings, the same leader can perform both functions, but it is still true that the heavy lifting of transition is done in the endings and the neutral zone and that a shift occurs as the new beginning takes place. That new beginning simply makes manifest the identity and purpose that were discovered and created in the wilderness—changes that were made possible by the letting go of the old ways that launched the transition and that is symbolized in Exodus by "leaving Egypt."

Index

About the Author

William Bridges is a preeminent authority on change and managing change in the workplace. A former literature professor, he was trained at Harvard, Columbia, and Brown, where he received his Ph.D. in American civilization in 1963. He initiated his own career change to become an adviser and consultant, founding William Bridges & Associates in 1981 to help organizations and individuals deal more successfully with transition.

William Bridges's assistance has been utilized in several hundred organizational mergers, reorganizations, leadership changes, and cultural shifts by companies including Pacific Bell, Baxter Healthcare, Intel, Kaiser Permanente, Proctor & Gamble, Hewlett-Packard, the U.S. Forest Service, Chevron Corporation, Saudi Aramco, Transamerica, Stanford University, *USA Today,* Shell Petroleum (London), the Australian Defence Forces, Astra-Zeneca Pharmaceuticals, and Thrivent Financial. The *Wall Street Journal* has listed him among the top ten independent executive development presenters in the United States. For more information on his publications and services, see his website, www.wmbridges.com, or contact:

William Bridges & Associates
38 Miller Avenue, Suite 12
Mill Valley, CA 94941
Telephone: 415-381-9663
Fax: 415-381-8124
E-mail: wmbridges@wmbridges.com